FINANCING YOUR BUSINESS

Books in the "Run Your Own Business" Series

Choosing a Legal Structure for Your Business
0-13-603366-0

Computerizing Your Business
0-13-603374-1

Day-to-Day Business Accounting
0-13-603358-X

Financing Your Business
0-13-603382-2

Managing Your Employees
0-13-603341-5

Promoting Your Business with Free (or Almost Free) Publicity
0-13-603390-3

Financing Your Business

Iris Lorenz-Fife

Prentice Hall
Englewood Cliffs, New Jersey 07632

Library of Congress Cataloging-in-Publication Data

Lorenz-Fife, Iris.
    Financing your business / Iris Lorenz-Fife.
       p. cm.
    Includes bibliographical references.
    ISBN 0-13-603382-2
    1. Small business—United States—Finance. 2. Business
enterprises—United States—Finance. I. Title.
HG4027.7.L67   1997
658.15′92—dc21   96-39730
                                          CIP

Printed in the United States of America

Printing 10 9 8 7 6 5 4 3 2 1

ATTENTION: CORPORATIONS AND SCHOOLS

Prentice Hall books are available at quantity discounts with bulk purchase for educational, business, or sales promotional use. For information, please write to: Prentice Hall Career & Personal Development Special Sales, 113 Sylvan Avenue, Englewood Cliffs, NJ 07632. Please supply title of book, ISBN number, quantity, how the book will be used, date needed.

PRENTICE HALL
Career & Personal Development
Englewood Cliffs, NJ 07632
A Simon & Schuster Company

ISBN 0-13-603382-2

Prentice-Hall International (UK) Limited, *London*
Prentice-Hall of Australia Pty. Limited, *Sydney*
Prentice-Hall Canada, Inc., *Toronto*
Prentice-Hall Hispanoamericana, S.A., *Mexico*
Prentice-Hall of India Private Limited, *New Delhi*
Prentice-Hall of Japan, Inc., *Tokyo*
Simon & Schuster Asia Pte. Ltd., *Singapore*
Editora Prentice-Hall do Brasil, Ltda., *Rio de Janeiro*

Gianni Lorenzini
a source of ongoing support.

Contents

3   Doing Business with a Little Help from Your Friends   *25*

4 Banking on Bankers   *41*

5 Getting the Bank on Your Side   *52*

6 All Loans Are Not Created Equal   *62*

16 Future Expansion   *164*

17 Planning for Long-Term Capital Expenses   *175*

Acknowledgments

Bringing a book from idea to finished product involves a great many people. Some contribute a small item that proves to have great value, others volunteer inordinate amounts of time, effort or support. My thanks to Donna Albrecht for bringing the project together, and to Roger Bel Air for always being a source of banking wisdom.

Many bankers, venture capitalists and private investors gave freely of their advice and expertise—I appreciate the input of each and every one of them.

Then there are the small-business owners who have shared their stories with me. These men and women have told me of their most embarrassing mistakes just because "my experience may help someone else avoid this problem." I wish every one of them prosperity and satisfaction from their businesses.

But the unsung heroes of the small-business world are those government workers who so often are automatically given a bad rap. I know this book could not have been written without the thoughtful, courteous, willing and knowledgeable assistance of the many men and women who are employed by our federal and state governments to administer the programs providing assistance to small-business owners. Whether in the Washington headquarters of SCORE, the San Francisco Regional SBA office, a Florida SBDC, or any of the hundreds of other locations throughout the country, these people are the best. I've called on them most recently to review the material for this book, but I've known their assistance over many years of writing for small-business owners. My experience has convinced me that small businesses are in excellent hands when they turn to a government agency for assistance.

Introduction

There is a point in each of our lives when we become adults. It's often a time of trial when we come upon an innate knowing that we *will* meet whatever challenges we are destined to face. The events around us may not reflect the fact that we have taken that single step from being, simply, grown-up to being adult; but the step is taken, and even if a crisis continues to worsen it will soon become apparent that we can now face the situation with integrity and courage. Indeed, even if we lose that particular war, it will be apparent that this new-formed adult will always meet the world with a different face than before.

There is a point in each business's life when it becomes a viable entity. In months and years it may still be a startup or may have long since aged to "established," but in a certain, probably brief and perhaps momentary, lapse of time it passes from vulnerability to viability. It isn't just money, or expertise, or even time but some combination of all those and more that amounts to the fact that the business will survive and grow and prosper and weather its storms and nurture its employees and serve its customers whether or not its owner stays at the helm.

Parents, if they are favored by the gods, may be present when a child becomes an adult, may even recognize what is happening. But with a person or a business it's more likely that we look back and say, "Oh, somewhere between May and June last year, when we were dealing with … I knew things were different."

An entrepreneurial friend said, "I thought I could give my business three years—36 months—and then I'd know whether I was going to be successful or not. As I reached the third anniversary I realized I might have to wait five years, and I no longer thought I could mark the date when I'd know on my calendar! Recently, I realized that during a recent period when we were all too busy to be aware of what was happening it seems like we received, collectively, an infusion of wisdom. Since then the business has had its own personality, separate from us. Before, it was my business, I'm the owner and founder, but now it belongs to all of us and anyone who ever comes to work here, and we belong to it. It's become an independent entity."

There was a point at the turn of the decade from the seventies to the eighties when the U.S. economy made a similar transition. We entered the decade of the eighties with much pessimism and much optimism and mighty little insight into the momentous change that had occurred; a change that literally spun America's business base on its heels and faced it in a new direction.

Only in retrospect can we see that at the cusp of the eighties we finally transitioned from being a declining industrial and manufacturing based economy, to being an economy based on emerging entrepreneurialism and technology-driven growth.

Only in retrospect can we see that America's businesses had passed from increasing vulnerability to increasing viability; and that the mantle of leadership was passing from the CEOs of Fortune's top companies to the shoulders of thousands of energetic, visionary citizens.

Why do we pinpoint the change to the end of the seventies? One reason is that 1979 saw the peak of employment by the Fortune 500's largest U.S. industrial corporations. Since then, their employee base has dropped from a peak of 16 million to a current 12 million. But since then, while four million people handled the elimination of their jobs with America's largest and finest, 24 million people became part of the country's small-business base, as employees of the strongest job-creating force our country has known. And this force has been generated by the diverse energies of entrepreneurial men and women.

Some of the other milestones noted in a recent Small Business Administration (SBA) report include the fact that American businesses have a "birthrate" that is three times higher than other industrial nations. Plus, in 1979 the volume of shares traded on the New York Stock Exchange was double that traded on NASDAQ, which in 1994 exceeded its rival for the first time. (Most of the entrepreneurial ventures that become part of the public equity market do so through initial public offerings on the over-the-counter market.) Moreover, a decade ago technology-related industries generated a twentieth of U.S. gross domestic product, but now they generate more than a ninth. And in 1994 and 1995 the World Economic Forum and the International Institute for Management and Development cited the U.S. as the world's most competitive economy.

At the end of 1979 many people saw only decline ahead and wondered how the country could survive. But at the beginning of 1980 many more saw opportunity for growth ahead, and they have led the way. Inevitably certain names have emerged and are looked to as the visionary embodiment of entrepreneurialism, but perhaps more than in any other time in our economic history the credit really belongs to the thousands of invisible men and women who put their money and their energy behind their dreams and in doing so changed the country's economy.

As a member of the latest generation of such entrepreneurs, you can reap the benefits of two decades of entrepreneurial wisdom. In this book you will not only learn how to finance your business, but how to master those financial strategies that will enable your dream to become a business, and your business to come of age, with the least compromise and the most grace.

1

Planning for Profits

Money! Whether you need $5,000 to equip a home office, $50,000 to outfit a lunch truck, or $5 million to expand a manufacturing plant, you probably need at least five times as much as you have. Perhaps the most daunting aspect of any new business idea is how much it will cost. In fact, the only good news about the fear entrepreneurs have of not being able to finance their business ventures adequately is that most of your potential competition will give up when they realize business financing is not a snap!

You won't, of course. You're already committed to finding the answers you need, and you have in your hands the means to make your business venture profitable. Whether you would like to begin a new business (a startup), expand an existing business, or seek additional financing to carry your business through a cash-flow crisis or an economic recession, you'll find the answers here.

Financing your business profitably, and for profitability, requires a combination of attitude, skills, and knowledge.

ATTITUDE

The A word has taken a beating in the last year or so, but approaching financing with the right attitude is too important to ignore. No, we're not expounding a pie-in-the-sky belief where all you have to do is have faith in your idea and someone will finance it. But we are advocating a positive approach to financing that manifests itself in friendly, courteous behavior toward financing professionals from accountants and bankers to attorneys and venture capitalists. The attitude we advocate requires you to assume that these people are willing to be your partners in ventures that are mutually profitable.

Both new and established business owners accept that their accountants and attorneys want their businesses to be profitable so that they can continue as clients. But a surprising number of first time entrepreneurs think that bankers and venture capitalists are out to get them, to make a profit for the banker at the borrower's expense.

This book assumes that both lenders and borrowers need to profit from their transactions in order to continue doing business and are therefore motivated to seek win-win solutions. We hold this attitude because extensive research has shown it to be true.

Throughout this book you'll find attitude tips—advice on how to approach potential lenders and investors. They are as important as the skills explained and the information imparted.

SKILLS

Every small-business owner who wants to convince a lender or investor that his or her enterprise is worth putting money into has to master specific skills. The bad news is that frequently these are the skills that many small-business owners lack.

Surveys show that over the last twenty years the majority of people starting new businesses have either sales or technical backgrounds. People with "technical skills" turn out specific products or services: Bakers open bakeries, plastics engineers open molding factories, and human resource managers open temporary personnel agencies. Admittedly, during the last few years an increasing number of people with middle management experience have left corporations to open their own enterprises, but few technical, management, or sales-oriented people have the necessary financial skills when they first go into business for themselves.

According to the Small Business Administration (SBA), most business failures can be attributed to lack of financial management. *You either learn these skills, or your business goes under.* This book will cover the financial management skills most directly related to obtaining financing. For a thorough understanding of the subject we strongly recommend *Day-to-Day Business Accounting* from this series.

When it comes to financing, the adage "If you fail to plan you are planning to fail" is at its truest. And you cannot plan the success—profitability—of your business unless you understand and can use financial tools.

KNOWLEDGE

The third essential in making a success of your venture is knowing where money is available and how to present your business in the best possible light. That's essentially what *Financing Your Business* is all about.

No matter what the prevailing economic conditions are, there is always money available for the business owner who can demonstrate an ability to pay back the lender or investor and to continue operating profitably. It's important to understand that proven profitability is the key skill you must demonstrate in order to obtain financing. A banker* speaking to his local chamber of commerce recently said, "Bankers are not in the business of making loans. They are in the business of making a profit, the same as each of you. You do it by providing a service or product, we do it by making loans."

If you think of financing as supplying a product (money) as a means of making a profit, you'll realize that bankers and investors are not very different from your suppliers and clients. They, too, are people with whom you can negotiate mutually prof-

---

*In researching this book we interviewed knowledgeable bankers, consultants and investors from across the country. Quotes attributed to "a banker" or "an investor" are an individual's own words, but are not quoted unless other bankers or investors agreed.

itable transactions; and while the tools and rules are different, the need to continue doing business together is just as certain.

PROFITS IMPRESS BANKERS

Even before you open your business you will have a "loss"—a negative flow from your bank account. Still, you must think "profits" from day one.

First, follow the expenditure rule of thumb: The amount you should spend to open your business is in direct proportion to the amount of experience you have in managing a small business. If this is your first year in your first business, you should keep your expenses as low as possible. Cut corners on everything but the actual product or service you are providing. In the beginning, paint and second-hand desks are much cheaper than interest on bank loans.

Plus, the more you stretch your startup capital the more impressed your banker will be, and your customers won't care as long as what they see is inviting and what they buy is good value.

Second, get your banker involved from the beginning. Select a bank you are comfortable with, meet your banker, and assure him or her that your relationship will be profitable for the bank because you either know, or will learn, how to manage your business profitably.

"It's fine to take your initial business plan into a banker and say, 'Here's what I want to do, and this is what I think I need, but I'm not sure. What do you think?'" says a banker. "This approach will move you and your banker away from an adversarial relationship and toward a partnership approach of figuring out how to make the business happen."

As you work with your banker, you will realize that bankers refer to different types of *capital* for different purposes. It may seem that if you can show a banker that you can repay a loan, then it should not matter how you use the money. But it does matter. Bankers want to assess for themselves whether the way you plan to use the loan will increase your business's profits. Furthermore, their expertise can make them excellent advisers for new and established business owners.

Third, you must track every dollar that goes out or comes into your business, starting with the very first day you make a purchase on behalf of your new venture. It's not difficult to carry a small notebook in which to track expenses and income on a daily basis. Keep track of **capital expenditures** (the permanent items that will not be sold or consumed in the course of business), **general expenses** (the items that are consumed but don't contribute directly to your product or service, such as rent, stationery, and cleaning supplies), **supplies** (the items that go into your product or service), and **income**.

You, and your banker, will expect to pay for capital expenses over a period of years, but from the very beginning you should think of covering a portion of that expense with each month's profits. **General expenses** are usually monthly items (including one-twelfth of such items as insurance), and if you are purchasing bulk **supplies** you need to estimate the amount you are using each month.

TRACKING YOUR PROFITABILITY

If you have never kept track of profit, here's a quick and easy way to do so:

	Sample month	Sample month
+ Income received from sales/services	$100.00	$100.00
− Less cost of supplies consumed	− 10.00	− 20.00
= Equals gross* profit	= 90.00	= 80.00
− Less general expenses	− 50.00	− 80.00
= Equals operating profit	= 40.00	= −.−
+ Plus other income	+ 10.00	+ 10.00
− Less other expenses	− 20.00	− 20.00
= Equals net* profit (or loss) before taxes	= 30.00	=(10.00)

*Probably everyone confuses gross profit and net profit at some time. Think alphabetically, G comes before N, so gross profit is figured earlier in the calculation than net profit.

Of course, you need to be more sophisticated about your bookkeeping than this. But even owners of many large corporations personally track capital expenses, general expenses (or overhead), supplies, and income in order to keep their own estimates of how well their companies are doing.

CHECKLIST: ARE YOU PREPARED FOR BUSINESS SUCCESS?

- [ ] Do I have good perseverance, or do I prefer to wait for opportunities to come along?
- [ ] Do I give up easily, or do difficulties just make me stubborn?
- [ ] Am I a loner, or do I like to get people involved in my projects?
- [ ] Am I prepared to enable others to make a profit as I make money?
- [ ] Do I always have to win, or do I have a win-win attitude?
- [ ] What is my background: technical, sales, management, financial?
- [ ] Where am I weakest?
- [ ] How do I assess my financial skills? Do I know how to figure (or even read) profit-and-loss statements, balance sheets, business ratios?
- [ ] Do I always keep my checkbook balanced?
- [ ] Am I willing to keep my expenses in proportion with my experience?
- [ ] Do I know the difference between capital and general expenses and supplies?
- [ ] Can I define gross profit and net profit?
- [ ] Do I understand how to keep a simple profit-and-loss statement?
- [ ] Am I willing to learn what I don't know?
- [ ] Do I expect my business to be profitable?
- [ ] What are our monthly general expenses?
- [ ] What portion of the cost of producing our project is for supplies?
- [ ] What is our monthly gross income?
- [ ] What is our monthly net income?
- [ ] How quickly did I find the answers to the questions on our finances?

2

An Overview of Business Money

KNOW WHAT YOU NEED

When Alan Bridges* invented a new type of corkscrew—the Wine Pop—he estimated his start-up manufacturing costs would be close to $50,000 and set about the task of raising that money. In the beginning Bridges did everything right. He attended Service Corps of Retired Executives (SCORE) classes for guidance on writing a business plan, hired an accountant to review it, and even got advice from a college buddy who was a banker in another state.

Six months later Bridges still didn't have his financing and says, "I felt I had started a business of raising money, instead of a business of manufacturing Wine Pops. I wasn't getting my product produced or marketed. I decided the business plan with hypothetical figures was a bunch of baloney, because to an investor the only pertinent question is, 'Will people buy it?'"

Bridges realized he needed to answer just two questions: "How much do I really need to get the Wine Pop launched?" and

*Over the last ten years the author has talked with hundreds of small-business owners from all over the country. In appreciation of their frankness we have changed names and identifying details to protect their privacy.

"What is the least I can spend to demonstrate that there is a market for the Wine Pop—that it's a viable product that's worth a $50,000 investment?"

Bridges reviewed his business plan and figured the answer to both questions was $5,000. Within days he had a home-based manufacturing business in operation, within a month he had shipped his first orders, and within six months the Wine Pop plant was financed.

Initially Bridges made one of those mistakes that are most common among neophyte entrepreneurs: He thought that raising money for his venture would be relatively easy. But not until he could prove that people would buy his product, and had used the financial tools covered in Chapter 10, "Negotiating the Best Loan," to show its potential for profit, could he interest anyone in financing his business.

EIGHT APPROACHES TO FINANCING

The range of financial sources willing to fund businesses is actually quite broad. Whether your enterprise is a startup or a well-established company, whether it's home based or has a commercial location, there are interested lenders and investors. Nevertheless, different types and sources of capital are usually directed to specific niches, and to choose the right financing for each stage of your business you must understand these common financial sources and how they interact. Here is an overview of those sources:

1. Your Assets

Despite all the advice to make your fortune by using other people's money, *you* will have to provide a substantial portion of whatever startup or expansion capital your business needs. "I expect to see the business owner contribute more than half the needed capital," says a commercial banker. "And if the business is a startup, I also want a lot of collateral, such as a deed of trust against a piece of real estate." Both bankers and investors will compare the amount of money you decide you can afford to commit to the venture with the amount needed to avoid jeopardizing its future through undercapitalization. If you are not willing to commit a substantial portion of the needed financing, most lenders and investors will assume either that you are not really optimistic about your business's success, or that you are not willing to stay with the venture if the going gets tough; and they'll also decline to be part of it.

As you assess your available assets—from the amount in your bank or money market funds, to stocks and bonds, to the equity in your house—don't assume you need to exhaust these funds before borrowing, or that this is the best way to stay out of debt. If, for instance, you cash in your certificates of deposit or sell your stock when the market dips, you might take an unnecessary loss, because for many bankers these assets have greater value when left intact and used as collateral for a loan.

You can also show commitment to your venture, especially if it's a startup, by significantly reducing your personal living expenses or taking a second, part-time job in the six to twelve months before starting your new business.

2. Family and Friends

The most common source of secondary startup and expansion capital is made up of family and friends. They may be eager to be part of your success. They may be gratified to be involved as full- or part-time employees, or they may be delighted to both mentor and partially finance your business. Family and friends invest in you, the business owner, rather than the product or service.

Funding from family and friends may be in the form of **subordinated loans** (meaning they are paid back after any bank loan), **equity investments** (where a return is not expected for several years), or **partnership agreements** (where the partners agree to split profits according to a formula that weighs capital, expertise, and the time and energy devoted to the enterprise.) Robert J. Gaston, author of *Finding Private Venture Capital for Your Firm*, advises new business owners to keep friendly funders happy by providing them with the same detailed business plans, and by signing the same legal agreements, that you would use with any other investors.

3. Business Angels

Outside equity financing for small business comes from two sources: the visible venture capital companies and the invisible private venture capitalists who are increasingly referred to as "business angels." According to the Small Business Administration (SBA), the visible segment consists of about 500 venture capital firms that are currently investing about $4 billion annually in some 3,000 ventures. In contrast, the invisible segment is conservatively estimated at 250,000 business angels who invest between $10 and $20 billion *each year* in over 30,000 businesses. Of equal interest to small-business owners is the fact that while venture capital companies prefer later-stage deals in the $2-3 million bracket, business angels will provide seed and startup funding from $100,000 to $1 million.

On the downside, the SBA estimates that the 30,000 business who are receiving angelic dollars represent only 60 percent of the 50,000 businesses in need. Other sources estimate that America's entrepreneurs need about $60 billion of patient, high-risk value-added equity capital each year. Businesses typically need these funds in two stages: first at the seed and startup stage to cover the research and initiation of the business, then to fuel established companies that are growing faster than their ability to generate cash from sales will support.

Balanced against the funding shortfall, we have an SBA estimate that there are probably five to ten times as many potential business angels who have not yet committed themselves.

Clearly, business angels are, and will remain, the largest single source of external risk capital for small businesses, whether they are local business owners with investment cash or individual millionaires willing to risk substantial capital on ventures with high-return potential.

Locally business angels come from your extended network. They are the men and women who have money to invest and a desire to do so in their local communities. Entrepreneurs value them as much for their wisdom as for their money, which suggests that the best way to find a business angel is to look for a mentor.

4. Customer, Supplier, and Seller Financing

The customers and clients you do business with might also be reliable sources of funding. For example, if your company has attracted a substantial order from a large corporation because you can meet its specifications at a discounted price, the client may be willing to make an advance payment, or deposit, for you to use to purchase supplies. In some industries this is a standard practice.

Suppliers are frequently willing to extend their credit terms from a typical thirty days to ninety days, especially if you are building your stock in anticipation of a seasonal selling period or to meet a large order. But if you want extended terms, be sure to request them before placing your order, not when it's due for payment.

Suppliers of major equipment, especially specialized machinery, have such a ready market for used equipment that they can usually offer competitive financing. Unless their interest rates and terms are really poor compared to your bank, this is probably the best way to finance these purchases. You may be able to get a service contract included in the price because it's in their interest to maintain the equipment. The time span of their loan should be based on the equipment's ability to pay for itself and, as an added bonus, this kind of arrangement spreads the financing risk—something your banker will favor.

If you're buying an established business, ask if the seller will finance at least that portion of the price that represents goodwill. If the seller is reluctant to help with the financing, try to find out if he or she has a genuine need for the capital, or if he or she doubts that the business can pay off the loan.

Some franchise companies will provide financing, others have a company policy not to be involved in financing new franchises. Nevertheless, a reputable company should know what assistance is available in the form of direct loans and investments in your area.

5. Banks and Bankers

There are two basic types of bank financing. The most useful for any business is the **line-of-credit**, which can be drawn on to an agreed-upon limit in return for minimum monthly payments. Your Visa or MasterCard is an example of a personal line-of-credit, usually with a rather high interest rate. Some business owners simply commit one of their personal charge cards to business purchases until the business has a sufficient track record to have its own line-of-credit approved.

The second type of bank loan is a **fixed-asset loan**. These loans may be unsecured, or secured by business assets, such as equipment and machinery which are then documented as the loan's collateral. Generally bankers expect new equipment to generate the income needed to pay for itself.

startup entrepreneurs usually put bank financing at the top of their lists, but established business owners realize that bankers are not risk takers. Bankers want to see managers with experience in both the business and the industry, a track record that shows the loan will be paid off in time, and at least two reliable sources of repayment. For a banker to consider a startup, the management team would have to have extensive experience in the industry and strong skills in all areas needed by the new enterprise; a good business plan is a must, and "friendly funds" would be a plus.

"If other people are interested in the venture, enough to put their own money into it, and if it was already well funded, then we would at least consider lending the difference between the equity cash and the projected financial needs," says one banker.

When it comes to home-based businesses the situation is even worse than for startups. Regrettably bankers are trained to assess traditional businesses and often don't consider home-based businesses to be serious ventures. To overcome this resistance you must package yourself and your concept as professionally as you are able. For instance, always see your banker by appointment, wear a business suit, and bring meticulously prepared documents with you. During the meeting, draw your banker's attention to the specific advantages of the home-based nature of your business, as well as to the good management practices you have shown by the way you handle your personal checking account, auto loan, and mortgage.

6. Federal Government Programs

Despite what you've heard, getting a Small Business Administration (SBA) loan is not much easier than getting a bank loan. Both banks and the SBA look for at least two reliable sources of repayment and want to see that the requested loan will contribute to the profitability of the business. However, if your banker has seriously considered your business but still turned it down, you should ask if the business would qualify for an SBA guaranteed loan. The advantage of an SBA guaranteed loan is that usually it's written for a longer term than a regular bank loan, and this extra repayment time can be the difference between a risky and a viable assessment in a banker's mind.

Under an SBA's guaranteed loan program, the government acts as a cosigner to your bank loan. In addition, the SBA often gives more weight to your business background than your banker might, increasing your chances of having the loan approved.

If your banker believes you would qualify for an SBA guaranteed loan, she or he will submit your application to the SBA and handle the paperwork. You will undoubtedly be asked for additional documentation, for collateral, and for more signatures on more pieces of paper than you thought were possible. Also an SBA loan will take longer to process, at least an additional month.

7. State and Local Government Assistance

Many states and local communities offer special programs directed to specific people or industries. Invariably they are designed to create jobs, and frequently they are intended to improve employment conditions in economically disadvantaged areas. State programs may be in the form of direct loans, low-interest bank loans, guaranteed loans, or deferred taxes.

8. Venture Capital

Also called **risk capital**, because investors share the risk that your company may not produce a profit, venture capital offers another funding opportunity. With venture capital, instead of guaranteeing to repay the funds (as with a loan), you offer the investor a share in your company and any resulting profits. The downside of using venture capital is that the investors may increase their investments until they own enough shares in your business to control it.

TYPES OF FINANCING

Soon after Alan Bridges began producing Wine Pops, he displayed them at a trade show. They were hot, and orders started arriving so quickly that Bridges was swamped within a week. He went shopping for a manufacturer who was willing to produce the basic units and give extended credit. Bridges found one, not just because his orders were from reputable, well-known trade distributors, but because he was honest about his need for credit.

Actually Alan Bridges needed several types of financing. **Seed money** enabled him to make a small stock and hire a display booth at a trade show. It got him started. Seed money usually comes from an entrepreneur's own resources or friends and family.

With some orders in hand, Bridges needed **inventory funds** to buy supplies; and with suitable collateral he may have gotten a bank loan on the strength of his orders.

In his first year, Bridges avoided needing **working capital** by arranging for a manufacturer to produce Wine Pops while he continued to market and ship from his home.

Of the $50,000 Bridges initially sought, 60 percent was for **capital investment** or **fixed-asset funding** (to pay for equipment and the fixtures needed to turn a rented warehouse into a production facility), 30 percent was for **working capital** or **operating capital** (to hire workers, pay rent and telephone charges, etc.), and 10 percent was for more **inventory** supplies. As a start-up, it was unlikely he would ever find a bank willing to lend all of the startup funds needed. Eventually, an equipment manufacturer financed the machine Bridges needed, his banker provided a **working capital line-of-credit** (for supplies and wages) on the strength of the increasing orders, and he found an angel with

investment capital to provide the difference between his own funds and the amount needed to convert the warehouse and cover the myriad other startup costs.

In that first year, Bridges learned to think of financial funding as a continuum. At one end is money that can be borrowed at a specific rate of interest, for a specific period of time, and to get it you must guarantee that you will repay it. At the other end is money that can be invested in your business, at a higher but more flexible cost, for a longer and more flexible period of time, but to get it you may have to give up complete control of your business. Between these extremes are a number of other funding sources with varying degrees of flexibility and varying costs.

FOUR CATEGORIES OF MONEY

Business consultants advise entrepreneurs to consider four categories of money as they plan the beginning or expansion of a business.

1. **Personal money** is needed for rent, food, clothes, transportation and some relaxation until your business is making a profit. Multiply your personal monthly costs by the number of months it will be until you can draw a salary from your business. Then double that total for the minimum you need in your personal money account before you get started. If you can put aside three times the amount you expect to need, do so; your business will grow faster if the profits can be put back into it.

2. **Capital investment money** is used to pay for the equipment you purchase, or the franchise or license you buy. You'll know if it's a capital investment if you can answer yes to the question, "Will there still be a tangible item that can be sold if my business fails?" Capital purchases can be used as collateral for the loans that are written to purchase them. Also, unless Congress makes drastic changes in the business tax laws, you will get an annual tax write-off by depreciating your major purchases over their lifetimes.

3. **Inventory capital** is needed to buy the products you plan to sell, or the parts that go into them and the wages paid to produce them. Inventory money covers those expenses that can be directly allocated to cost of goods sold in your bookkeeping.

4. **Working capital** supports your day-to-day operations. It pays for office supplies, wages of nonmanufacturing staff, rent, and advertising.

As you can see, each category of money has more than one name and, regrettably, we haven't covered them all yet! What's important is to realize that people who deal with financing—accountants, attorneys, bankers, business consultants, angels and investors—use different names according to what the money is being used for and how it is being provided. For now, if you have a clear idea of the different categories of money use, you'll be able to converse intelligently with those financial people and you can leave the special terms for later.

Three months after Alan Bridges started producing Wine Pops in his garage, he bumped into his banker at a chamber of commerce mixer. "How's the business going?" asked the banker, probably expecting a "good" or "so-so" response.

"Positively!" said Bridges. "We are now paying the manufacturer within forty-five days of delivery and expect to break even by the end of next month."

"What most impressed me," said the banker, "was not the volume of sales, the positive cash flow, or the early break-even date, but the fact that Bridges was keeping track of this information on a daily basis. I didn't tell him, but I knew then that we would be making a loan to Wine Pops."

TO CHARGE OR NOT TO CHARGE?

Probably the most controversial way to finance a business's expenses is the charge card route. Everyone has read about such people as filmmaker Robert Townsend, who finished the blockbuster movie *Hollywood Shuffle* by using an $8,000 charge card line-of-credit. As a result of such stories, many people automatically think "charge card" when they consider starting a business. Yet others believe that if you can't find people who are willing to help you finance your business (from bankers to angels), then maybe it's an idea whose time has not yet come.

If only the answer were that simple!

Although using charge cards for business expenses certainly has a place in your business financing plans, relying on charge card financing for startup costs, working capital, or business expansion is not recommended. Nevertheless, there may be occasions when you decide it's the right thing to do.

Why Not to Use Charge Cards

- High Interest Rates. Charge card interest rates are among the highest you can pay. Interest of between 12 percent and 18 percent can eat up whatever profit you're making, and there's no point being in business if your expenses are crippling.

- Credit Rating Risk. If the only way you can finance major business expenses is by a personally guaranteed line-of-credit, you probably cannot afford the loss if your business doesn't make enough profit to pay these debts. It would be bad enough to have your business fail without having your credit rating destroyed as well.

- Discipline Required. Charge-card-itis is a major financial disease. Only you know whether you can restrict your charge card use to planned purchases and not succumb to the temptation to buy things for your business that are unplanned.

When It Makes Sense to Charge

- In Emergencies. If, for instance, a piece of equipment breaks down and you must have a replacement within hours, it can make very good sense to use your charge card. But if you cannot pay the full amount as soon as you receive the statement, you should definitely try to arrange seller or bank financing using the equipment as collateral.

- For Documentation. A charge card is sometimes the best method for documenting specific expenses. For instance, suppose you or an employee makes monthly sales trips involving hotels, meals, car rentals, photocopying, and so on. Keeping track of some of these amounts is tedious. By charging all items on the trip and paying the account as soon as you are billed, you have good documentation for your business expenses and the IRS.

- When You Firmly Believe That Your Business Venture Will Succeed. Perhaps you have the figures to support your belief, you are convinced that the principal reason for the bank's disinterest is that your business is not common enough to be easily evaluated, or you have a steady source of income that can pay off the credit card balances. (That steady source of income might be a working spouse, a part-time job, or investment income; it should be money that you and your family are willing to dedicate to getting your business off the ground.) If your confidence in the business is this unwavering, charging your business expenses might be a viable option.

HOW TO USE CHARGE CARDS IN BUSINESS

1. If you are going to use charge cards in your business, do research to determine which cards carry the lowest fees. For a card that is dedicated to specific expenses that will be paid off each month, you need plastic that does not carry an annual fee. However, if you would be willing to carry a credit card balance at any time, apply for cards with the lowest available interest rates, and do so months before you might need them.

2. Don't use the card for startup expenses. If you are at all prepared to carry credit card balances for business expenses, plan to use them at the twelve- to eighteen-month point, when almost every business finds itself in a credit crunch. Instead of using the card for startup expenses, we strongly recommend you defer launching your business until you have either accumulated the necessary cash or found outside financing.

3. Plan your cash and credit use carefully. If you decide to use plastic for business expenses, do so only for those purchases that you can charge. Keep your cash for the purchases where the seller will not take plastic. Yes, you can draw cash from a charge card account, but you will pay a premium when you do. Most charge card companies charge a cash advance fee plus interest from the day of the cash draw; you don't need to burden your business with these extra fees.

4. Keep careful records. Provided a charged amount is for a legitimate business expense, both the charge and any interest paid on it is tax deductible. Good documentation will enable you to take, and defend, your charge card deductions.

- Use different cards for your business and personal charges.
- At the time of the charge, write on the charge slip what was charged and a description of its business purpose.

CHECKLIST: WHAT FINANCING IS BEST FOR YOUR BUSINESS?

☐ How much financing does my business need at this time?

☐ What are the alternative amounts? What's the difference between the lean and mean plan and the optimal plan?

☐ What personal assets can I tap to finance my business? Investment, savings or special purpose accounts? Home equity? Stocks and bonds? Other?

☐ Do I need seed money, inventory funds, working capital, or capital investment funds? In which proportions will I need these funds and over what time periods?

☐ Do I need a loan or an investment?

☐ What portion of my financial needs would best be met by a line-of-credit, and what portion by a term loan?

☐ Do I understand the difference between angel, banking, and venture capital financing?

☐ Who among my family and friends might be interested in funding the amount I need? With a loan? With an investment?

☐ Who in my business community invests (or might invest) in other businesses?

☐ Would I be willing to run my business as a partnership with an investor? Under what conditions?

☐ Would asking for a deposit with an order be a reasonable option in my business?

☐ Under what conditions might suppliers be willing to provide long-term credit?

☐ If I borrow for inventory, will I still make a profit when the cost of the loan is added to the cost of the goods?

☐ If this loan is for machinery or major equipment, does the manufacturer or distributor offer competitive financing?

☐ Is it better financial sense to borrow now or to wait until the business can finance the expense?

☐ If I don't make the purchase, how will it affect the growth of my business?

☐ Is using charge cards something I could comfortably do? If so, what are the parameters within which I will make charges?

☐ What will I still owe if my business goes under?

☐ How can I handle this debt so that my business is not over-strained?

3

Doing Business with a Little Help from Your Friends

Three years ago, Carla Edwards opened Elegant Exteriors in an old country town. Her main-street store carries everything to enhance the outsides of her customer's homes, from Victorian molding and French window shutters to ornamental patio trees and upscale outdoor furniture. Elegant Exteriors has done well for Edwards, but she has realized that it would do much better if located in the county seat, so wants to open a second, larger store there. She has found the ideal location and thought the bank would be eager to provide financing on a proven plan.

"But money is in such short supply," she sighs. "I've reworked my business plan three different ways, but my available capital won't stretch to the stock and staff I need for that size store. Yet the location is ideal, and if I take too small a facility or don't have a good location, I could limp along for years without getting off the ground." Edwards points to the inventory figures and laughs wryly, "One banker would be willing to advance inventory money after I generate six months of sales in the new location. But how can I sell inventory without inventory? I guess I need an angel!"

Sound familiar? Carla Edwards's business plan is well done and she's proven her market knowledge with her existing store, but conservative bankers are viewing her new store as a startup rather than an expansion of her existing business.

FINANCING CONTINUUM

Edwards's situation is proof of the *financing continuum* discussed in Chapter 2. Banks are at the conservative end, so you have to guarantee repayment and bankers seemingly won't believe anything they can't prove themselves. A loan to improve **freehold** (to refurbish an empty store and create an inviting place to shop) doesn't provide a banker with collateral to repossess if necessary. Even if it did, bankers want to stay out of the secondhand equipment business, so they would still insist on a proven and secure cash flow to pay off the debt.

At the other end of the financial continuum we find risk financing in its purest form: venture capitalists who invest in your business and share the risks of failure and the rewards of success. But a venture the size of Carla Edwards's is just too small to interest these firms, who prefer to invest large amounts over a period of stepped expansion. In addition, venture capitalists frequently want a 51 percent share of a retail business so that they have a controlling interest. This gives them the power to intervene, perhaps even forcing the owner to sell if the venture capitalists want to pull out before the business has generated enough money for the owner to buy them out.

This leaves the entrepreneur the middle of the financing continuum where there really are angels!

THERE REALLY ARE ANGELS

Angels are men and women who are willing to act as guardian angels to small businesses. According to the Small Business Administration (SBA), informal investment capital—from angels—is the largest source of external equity capital for small businesses. Today angels can be divided into two substantial groups: Those who are millionaires and invest larger amounts in riskier ventures with greater potential for profit, and those successful entrepreneurs who tend to invest in more stable ventures in their own communities.

Bill Gates is the outstanding example of the first group; for reasons he describes as "intellectual as well as financial" he has bankrolled several startup ventures in the biotech field. Gates is part of that group which in a 1986 cover story, *U.S.News & World Report* described as a typical self-made entrepreneur millionaire. Two years later *Time* magazine estimated there were two million millionaires in the country, and that 90 percent of them had earned their fortunes by starting their own companies.

In Robert Gaston's survey for the SBA, he found that small angels were investing nearly $6 out of every $10 in very small firms with less than four employees and sales of under $150,000. According to the SBA, these angels earn approximately $100,000 a year from their own mature businesses. An SBA survey of 435 informal angel investors found the following:

- The angels who invest in smaller companies are not millionaires; 31 percent had family incomes of less than $50,000; the median was $90,000.
- Angels will consider small investments; 21 percent were less than $10,000, while 64 percent were less than $50,000.
- Angels are usually entrepreneurs; 83 percent are either business owners or managers.
- Angels are usually older than the entrepreneurs they help; their median age was 47 years.
- Angels who invest in very small businesses are almost invisible, but are nevertheless the largest source of small-business financing in the country.

"Entrepreneurial angels can be our friends, neighbors, and acquaintances who are willing to take a gamble on a new small business," says an SBA spokesperson. Angels are as close as your family, your local business association, and the other businesses on your street. Admittedly, they are not easy to identi-fy—they don't wear halos and they tend to be inconspicuous.

Family Angels

Emotionally and physically, the angels nearest to you will proba-bly be members of your immediate family, and the family mem-ber most likely to be an angel is the one who owns, or has owned, a business. Such angels are highly advantageous to the entrepre-neurs they help. Because of the family connections, they are usu-ally quite generous with their time and are willing to explain fi-nancial ratios or help meet a production deadline. Plus, they frequently accept a lower anticipated return on investment (10 to 15 percent) than would satisfy other investors.

Friendly Angels

Close behind the family angel is the friend who knows you well enough to have faith in your sense of responsibility, clearhead-edness, creativity, ambition, and drive. This person's managerial and entrepreneurial experience is the same as the family angel's, and he well understands the trials (and delays in repayment) that a small business goes through.

Community Angels

Most angels won't be as physically and emotionally close to you; but they won't be very far away either. Nearly 70 percent of small-business angels are represented by the business own-ers and managers in an entrepreneur's local community. And although most such angels are white males, each year more women and minorities are represented in their numbers. For many, reaching out to small-business owners is a payback. They were helped by a similar businessperson in their startup years, and with success and business maturity they look for the opportunity to give back to their communities. As with family angels and friendly angels, community angels understand the trials a small business goes through and have practical wisdom to impart, as well as encouragement and financial assistance.

Internet Angels

Increasingly millionaire angels are turning to the Internet to find the ventures they want to invest in. They are identified by their:

- Initiating a trend to move more of their investments into relatively speculative investments. (The percentage of wealthy families making such a change is expected to grow from 20.7 percent in 1995 to 30.7 percent by 2000.)
- Ability to evaluate the commercial value of complex new products.
- Willingness to invest where the collateral is primarily the reputation of the founders and the technology and marketing teams.
- Willingness to invest up to $1 million.
- Willingness to invest seed and startup funds.
- Willingness to go outside their own geographic areas to make the investment they want.

ANGEL'S GOLD

Most angels offer investment capital rather than loans, or a combination of the two. For the angel, it's leveraged investing and for you it's solid, if creative, financing. For instance, you might trade a share of your business for $20,000 of new capital, a later loan of $20,000 from the angel, plus a third $20,000 in a bank loan that the angel cosigns or guarantees.

Because angels are usually extremely patient lenders and investors, payment on their loans may be delayed if the business has a poor quarter. There is also the chance that angels won't get all their gold back. For instance, if the business goes under, the angel will lose his or her investment; in fact, an angel's direct loan may be written so that in the event that the business fails, the loan won't be fully repaid. Because of these conditions, angel loans are described as "near-equity" capital.

There is another important reason for allowing angels to invest in your company. By forming partnerships with investors who are experienced entrepreneurs, you gain mentors during those years when you most need them. Because 85 percent of angels do not seek voting control, you need not fear that your investors will try to dictate to you, even if several of them are on your board of directors. Angels are motivated by the desire to help someone who is starting a company to avoid the problems they too clearly remember.

ANGELIC SEARCHING

Traditionally angels find the entrepreneurs they work with through word of mouth. They get referrals from their bankers, accountants, attorneys, and other business associates and friends. To attract them, tell your professional advisers—your accountant, attorney, business consultant, and banker, any one of whom could know several potential investors—that your business could include investment opportunities. Then network: Join your local chamber of commerce, business groups and trade associations. Talk about your plans and your interest in private financing. If you need more than $100,000 expand your search throughout your state and onto the Internet.

Community angels can actually include a broad range of people, from doctors and lawyers to retirees from the same type of business you want to start. If you meet someone with the following qualifications, you may be talking to a potential angel:

- Self-employed or managing a small company
- Between the ages of forty and fifty-five
- Earning between $40,000 and $100,000 a year
- Experienced in a similar or related business. (All levels of angels show a propensity for using their own business backgrounds to evaluate the products and services they consider financing.)

ATTRACTING ANGELS

When trying to interest a potential angel in your business, remember that your own personality and motivations are important considerations for potential investors. A survey to specify the characteristics angels are attracted to identified the following traits:

1. Drive to succeed—obsession to be successful
2. The mental discipline to direct and control that drive
3. A middle-class background and a belief that hard work will pay off
4. Or a background of poverty that has resulted in an "I'll show them" attitude
5. Willingness to work hard, for both material rewards and the satisfaction of the endeavor
6. Belief in the American dream
7. The ability to turn negatives into positives
8. A sense of guilt from letting parents or a spouse down, which results in a drive to succeed
9. In women: early maturity, a practical sense of purpose, and good contingency planning

These are not characteristics you can assume or learn if they are not already present. Nor are they characteristics that you can easily advertise. But when a potential investor asks about your own background, remember that this is the type of personal motivation he or she may be looking for.

Such characteristics can be demonstrated to potential investors through involvement in chamber of commerce or industry organization affairs. Membership on a visible committee is an ideal way to show your ability to get things done and to interact with people, as well as to demonstrate your drive. However, such community involvement must also demonstrate that you know how to allocate your time so that your own business (the angel's potential investment) does not suffer by your absence.

WHAT ANGELS DON'T WANT

According to the SBA survey, the average angel seriously considers a third of all the opportunities he or she discovers and invests in one-third of those considered. To attract your angel's attention, you need a practical business plan (use the loan application package described in Chapter 9, "Presenting Your Bottom Line," as a basis) that also addresses the small investor's special needs. Think about the person you wish to consider your plan, and put yourself in the investor's place: What would you want to know about the business before putting your money into the deal? The most common reasons angels give for rejecting investment opportunities are the following:

- I don't know the key people well enough. There isn't enough information in the package about the principal people, or those people haven't made themselves available for personal meetings.

- I don't think there is enough market potential for the product or service. The marketing figures may be nonexistent or unsubstantiated.

- The value of the equity being sold is too high for my requirements. The business plan does not provide for a variety of investment opportunities, such as equity or loan investments from one or more angels.

SET YOUR TERMS

One of the things a potential investor will look for in your business plan is the price you place on your company as an investment. Most angels look for an annual return of between 15 and 20 percent over four or five years. They can be tempted by lower returns if your deal has a low risk factor, just as surely as they will want higher returns if they foresee greater risk than normal.

Expected returns will also be influenced by cost of money. Private investors may expect returns of two, three, or four times what they could get in the stock market, depending on the riskiness of the venture and the strength of the market at the time you are making your pitch. To many angels, investing in a private company is much more than a way to diversify; they expect it to be less risky than the stock market in that they can use their personal business acumen to evaluate the risk and become involved as advisers to influence that risk.

Your business plan also needs to state how long you expect your angels to stay invested in your business and how they will leave. Although an angel might like to leave at his or her own discretion (for reasons having to do with the progress of the business or because of personal demands), you must protect your cash flow and your ability to stay solvent.

EXPAND YOUR BUSINESS PLAN

Your business plan should outline all of the issues the angel may wish to consider.

Financing

For an angel's thoughtful consideration, a business plan must include a clear description of anticipated financing from startup to maturity. You may be looking for just one angel at the beginning, but you should spell out the additional amounts and the number of investors to whom you are willing to sell equity.

Strategies

One of the problems angels report is that too often business plans are single-dimensional, assuming one, and only one, set of circumstances and responses. More sophisticated business plans include alternate strategies, such as "If the advertising plan doesn't generate such and such results, we will do this, and this, and then that." Angels like to see these alternatives because they provide information on the business venture and prove that you are sufficiently flexible to respond constructively to whatever happens.

Management

As suggested earlier, since angels often turn down businesses because the information given about the entrepreneurs doesn't demonstrate that they have the experience and talent to succeed, the personnel section of your business plan should contain enough personal history to fully describe each key person in your enterprise. Early in the angel's consideration of your business venture, you should also provide the opportunity for the angel and your key people to meet. Making yourselves directly available so that the angel can assess your character and motivations may be the difference between a committed and valuable partnership and no deal.

References

One angel we know actually asks for the names of two or three "enemies" who will give him an honest and unburnished account of your personal qualities. Certainly you should include the names of several disinterested associates who have worked with you on various projects and who have experienced your abilities to organize, inspire, and problem solve.

Be Optimistic

Don't be unduly modest when providing information that a potential angel will use to determine an investment decision. It's better to be bullish, without stretching the facts, on your firm's chances for growth, the talent and managerial experience of its key people, and why it is a good investment at the proposed price.

However, you also want to protect yourself against the full effect of Murphy's law. Be sure to include a disclaimer that says, for instance, that your projections are projections, that nothing is certain and that you are offering the opportunity to take part in a business with great potential. But there are no guarantees. If there were, you could go to a bank; you wouldn't need risk financing.

The SBA survey shows that angels actually prefer business startups and very young companies with lots of potential despite their greater risk.

WHEN ANGELS RESPOND

If your plan is rejected, you might ask the angel if he or she knows of someone else your business might appeal to. If your plan is accepted, you have some important negotiating to do. Each investment agreement should do the following:

- Spell out the amount of the investment
- Spell out the timing of the investment
- Say how long it will last
- Describe how the return will be calculated
- Detail how the investment will be cashed out
- Describe the degree of involvement each angel will have in the business, from board membership to part-time employment.

An equity investment agreement obligates the angel to provide either a specific amount of money at the signing of the agreement or serial investments over a more extended period of time. In return the angel receives a share, or portion of ownership, in the company. The most obvious point of negotiation is how much the angel will invest, and how much equity he or she will receive in return. Unfortunately, sometimes this discussion becomes the sole focus of the negotiations and some equally important points are ignored.

When entrepreneurs are unhappy with angels it is most frequently because their angels make them wait for funding. Sometimes the angel doesn't want to advance the next piece of an investment until, say, the business receives a major order. This type of holding back results in slow starvation, because the company is unable to continue a marketing program or buy supplies for small orders that would keep it going. From the entrepreneur's viewpoint, infusions of investment or loan cash should be set by the calendar rather than be tied to events. The former enables the entrepreneur to plan the growth of her or his company, the second strips that control.

When small-business owners sell a portion of their companies to angel investors, they can do so with or without giving up voting control. Suppose you take in nine investors and sell each of them a 10 percent share of the company; you could retain either 51 percent of the voting rights or just 10 percent. In other words, the angels could receive voting stock, nonvoting stock, or a combination of both. What's important is that you decide in advance how much control you are willing to relinquish.

Entrepreneurs are inclined to see themselves as the parents of their companies and to view angels as the midwives. As such, they assume that everyone will always agree that the parent is the right and proper person to raise the child. An entrepreneur who has given up company control in the belief that she or he is indispensable may find that this is not the case. Unless you own a patent separately from the business and have retained the control of that patent, or have a body of knowledge that can't easily be duplicated, or have a significant name-recognition value for the company, assume that it's always possible that a combination of recession and greedy angels could threaten your position as the company's manager *if* you give up voting control.

Of course, you can't expect angels to completely relinquish control of their investments under all circumstances. Most will have specific protection requests based on their experience, and most of those will be for either withdrawal of capital or change of management in certain dire situations. Minimize their effect on your ability to run your company as effectively as you can by making the situations in which these requests can be activated as specific as possible.

Perhaps the worst scenario for taking on private investors is to do so in dribs and drabs. If you, as the entrepreneur, sell a small percent of your company each time you need to raise more cash, you might find yourself working as an employee for what once was your own firm. Such a scenario won't come about if you have a long-term plan for the growth of your company, but it's the sort of thing that happens when you take a seat-of-your-pants approach to business management.

The most win-win results from negotiations tend to give the investors hope and expectation for high returns, while letting the entrepreneur control the business. You can reach that point by knowing where you want to take your business, by understanding its potential. If you want to create a $100 million company, you may only be able to do so with 10 percent ownership, but that's worth a lot more than 100 percent of a $1 million company.

HOW WILL THE INVESTMENT BE LEGALIZED?

Most angels prefer one of these options:

- Common stock—ordinary ownership shares in a corporation
- Partnership equity—ownership interest used in place of common stock when only a very small number of working owners are involved

When angels take a common stock position, the company issues private stock (an attorney with a business specialty can take care of this), which may or may not pay dividends. Whether an angel wants dividends or not will depend upon the angel's personal income and tax situation. Small-business owners using angel equity capital are better off not committing to pay dividends unless their firms are well established and are using this financing for the steady expansion of known products. If you commit to paying dividends on startup equity, for instance, you may find yourself with unhappy investors in the event of a bad quarter—instead of investors who are both patient and ready to take the risk of a higher, but less certain, return.

Partnerships can be limited or general. An angel who is involved in the day-to-day management of the company would be a general partner. As such, he or she would be equally responsible for the company's debts. Because each general partner is fully responsible for the debts of a company, most angels find limited partnerships preferable. They have no say in the management of the company, except as advisers, but nor can they be held responsible.

Some of the less desirable legal alternatives include the following:

- Convertible debentures—unsecured bonds that can be exchanged for stock, usually at the bondholder's option
- Convertible preferred stock—ownership shares that enjoy special privileges, usually regarding dividend payments that can be exchanged for common stock, again at the holder's option

- Notes with warrants—short-term debt instruments, usually due in less than five years, which carry provisions (warrants) allowing conversion into common stock under predetermined conditions, usually at the option of the noteholder

Although nothing is inherently wrong with any of the three alternatives—except their lack of simplicity—any offer from an angel requesting such a form should be carefully considered to ensure that it isn't the calling card of a devil.

BEWARE THE DEVIL IN ANGEL'S CLOTHING

More complicated offers may actually be from that perfidious person Robert Gaston describes as "a devil in angel's garb." A devil wants your business. A devil may start as an uninvolved board member who gradually infiltrates into the day-to-day management of the business. Or a devil may start as a corporate manager seeking only a position and an investment opportunity. This person may only want to help out now, but will be angling for control later.

Unfortunately, devils can be hard to differentiate from angels. Guard against them by examining your deal carefully to prevent an investor from parlaying current equity, or future loans to your company, into a controlling interest. Such a deal is not made in heaven.

Fortunately, most angels are what they seem to be: serious small investors. You have something valuable to offer, so choose your angel carefully. The right expertise might ultimately do more for your business's profitability than large amounts of potential cash. Also, because the investment goals and motivations of angels are so diversified, almost any business can find its own piece of heaven.

Finally, as the SBA enjoys pointing out: "The history of business in the U.S. is the history of equity financing. In today's entrepreneurial economy, creating quality jobs in globally competitive ventures is a chaotic, untidy process. However, corporate America endures precisely because it innovates, adapts and evolves."

CHECKLIST: ARE ANGELS RIGHT FOR YOU?

☐ If all financing could be arranged on a continuous line with one end labeled "risk" and the other end labeled "sure," where would bankers be? Angels? Venture capitalists? Family funds?

☐ How likely is it that I already know several angels, without having seen through their disguises?

☐ Who in my family fits the profile of an angel?

☐ Who else do I know who fits the profile of an angel?

☐ Who does, or could, mentor my business?

☐ Who do I know who may be able to refer me to an angel?

☐ What associations or meetings can I attend to meet potential angels?

☐ Do any of the descriptions under "Attracting Angels" fit me? If so, how could I demonstrate this to a potential angel?

☐ How can I describe my key people so that a potential angel would appreciate their suitability for a management role in my company?

☐ Can I prove the market potential for my product or service?

☐ Can I offer equity options in order to reach a win-win contract with an investor?

☐ What are the minimum, maximum, and ideal terms for investments in my company?

☐ Does my business plan present alternative strategies where the outcome of situations may vary?

☐ What references can I offer to a potential angel?

☐ Does my plan present my business optimistically yet realistically? Have I avoided any misleading statements?

☐ What stock options, partnerships, or voting control would work best for my business?

☐ What share of equity and control will I have to surrender?

☐ What collateral will I have to put up?

☐ What will I owe if my business goes under?

☐ What long-term financing do I need? Over the next year? Three years? Five years?

☐ When will I need funding again? What are the steps of my projected growth?

☐ Do I have a business attorney who is competent to advise me on angel contracts?

4

Banking on Bankers

The Hunts bought the Irish Bar & Grill from its original owner with the advice of an attorney and a CPA. "We knew better than to go into business without such professionals on our team," explained George, "but since the seller also did the financing we haven't had much reason to think about bankers."

"Actually," Felicity added, "we left the business's accounts where they were because that was convenient, and we left our own personal accounts at our bank for the same reason. We never considered that there would be a reason to have them at the same bank."

"Even worse," groaned George, "whenever we saw profits accumulating in the business account, we immediately drew them out and put them into a money market account."

Not until their Day of Disaster did the Hunts realize what mistakes they had been making. In the space of four hours they had to pay out three large amounts of cash: for a C.O.D. shipment of specialty wines and liquors, to get a fast replacement of a plate-glass window when a truck's brakes failed and it jumped the curb, and for the installation of a commercial dishwasher. And just a few days earlier Felicity had transferred most of the money in their business's bank account into their money market fund.

"Even when we realized it was payday and our staff would want to cash their checks, we didn't think it would be a problem," said George.

"I figured I'd just run over to the bank and explain to the manager what had happened," said Felicity.

"He'd cover the payroll checks, and within a couple of days there would be enough funds to cover the overdraft."

Felicity and George could hardly believe their ears when the bank manager, whom they'd never met before, said no. Within just a few minutes the Hunts recognized the need for a good business banker and for a good relationship with that banker.

Bankers still provide the basic, day-to-day financing for most businesses and without a good banker your business could permanently stall on any one of the many events that should be no more than minor obstacles.

GOOD BANKERS PROVIDE FOUR ESSENTIAL SERVICES

1. They provide the banking services you need, performed by people who work efficiently and courteously.
2. They write lines of credit and term loans when your business needs working capital and equipment.
3. They provide sound advice on business trends and expansion.
4. They focus on what may go wrong; their cynacism is an essential balance to entrepreneurial optimism.

FINDING THE BEST BANKERS

You already know that all banks are not created equal, so it should not be a surprise to learn that some bankers are better than others. Ex-banker and author Roger Bel Air maintains "There are more bad bankers than there are really good ones, and it's very important that you find the right banker for your business—someone you can relate to, someone who seems competent, who understands your needs and cares about you and your business. Your probability of getting money when you need it is much greater from that person."

BANKERS AND ENTREPRENEURS ARE DIFFERENT

Bankers and entrepreneurs share the desire to make a profit in a highly competitive marketplace, but that's where their similarities end and their differences begin.

Entrepreneurs are risk takers who see needs in the marketplace for them to fill with products and services.	Bankers are primarily concerned with preserving depositors' funds.
Entrepreneurs are optimists, looking for success and the riches it brings.	Bankers ask, first and last, "What can go wrong?"
Entrepreneurs are independent decision makers.	Bankers seek group consensus.
Entrepreneurs operate with minimal regulations.	Bankers operate in an industry that, despite deregulation, is tightly organized.
Entrepreneurs are leaders in charge of businesses.	Bankers are employed by bureaucratic organizations.
Entrepreneurs like to be in control.	Bankers often control the purse strings.
Entrepreneurs act.	Bankers advise.

BANKERS ARE HIERARCHICAL

Understanding a banker's viewpoint is just one aspect of building a relationship with your banker. You must also understand the bureaucracy in which your banker works.

Your banker's business card includes a title that indicates his or her position in the bank's hierarchy, a position that carries with it a specific dollar value of lending authority. A banker rises in the hierarchy by increasing his or her lending authority—the loan amount he or she can approve without consulting the person with the next level of lending authority.

Typically a loan officer at a branch bank might be able to approve loans up to $15,000; the vice president of the branch might have a lending authority of up to $30,000; while the branch manager might be able to write loans of twice that amount, or $60,000. When this small branch receives a loan request of more than $60,000, it would have to be forwarded to the bank's main office where several more levels of bank managers would be authorized to approve loans in amounts of, say, $100,000, $300,000, $600,000 and $1 million according to their seniority. Loans of up to $2 million would need the approval of either the executive vice president or the president of the bank, and anything above that would have to be presented to a committee for consideration. (Actual lending amounts vary by the size of the branch, the assets of the bank, the state, and whether the bank services mostly small or large accounts.)

However, your loan application for $80,000 to finance new equipment would not go directly to the manager authorized to approve loans up to that amount. Instead, you must present your application to your own banker, who will review it and make an initial decision. That determination will be based on how well he or she knows you, values your business, believes your business can repay the loan, and trusts your intention to do so. Based on this criteria, your banker will either turn down your application or forward it to the banker of next higher rank for a similar review. In most banks this process of independent determination by each loan officer in a hierarchy continues until the loan application reaches an officer with the appropriate degree of lending authority.

SHOPPING FOR A BANKER

To find a banker, begin by making a list of the business associates whose recommendations you respect. Presumably there's your attorney, your CPA, and selected members of your trade association and the local chamber of commerce.

When you talk to these people, ask about specific services they have used. Ask how their loan requests were handled and how long it took to get specific loan amounts approved. Remember that just because one person is turned down by a particular banker doesn't mean that banker should be eliminated from your consideration, because so much depends on the quality of the individual loan application. Get the opinions of several people.

If you are new to a community and really don't have any personal recommendations to consider, start by meeting with the bankers at those local banks that advertise for business clients. Such banks are more likely to have the business services you may need, such as secured after-hours cash deposits, international letters of credit for exporting, Small Business Administration (SBA) loan guarantees, and so forth, than will banks that focus on making consumer car loans and home mortgages. Frequently community banks are more business oriented, and it stands to reason that you will benefit from their putting a higher priority on growing local businesses.

Take the time to meet with several bankers to discuss your business and the banks' services—finding the right banker is an important decision. In evaluating each banker on how well he or she will meet your needs ask yourself if the banker has done the following:

- Shown a sincere interest in you and your business?
- Demonstrated common sense and the ability to see the overall concept?
- Proved to have the ability to communicate clearly without using financial jargon?
- Had the confidence to recognize that financial reports are valuable, but that they do not reveal everything that affects a business's success?
- Pointed out the trends your financial statements demonstrate about your company and suggested how they may affect you?
- Returned your phone calls promptly?
- Personally visited your business to better understand your operation and your financial needs?

- Looked for creative ways to finance your business needs and still provide adequate protection for the bank, rather than simply rejecting your loan request?

- Given direct answers to questions about loan amounts, terms, and so on? Look for the banker whose explanations go beyond simply saying, "The bank's policy is to make loans of $50,000 and up." (While it's true that many banks don't like writing loans for small amounts because they take the same amount of paperwork as larger loans, which makes them un-economical to process, it's also true that bankers who are looking for growth businesses can and will make loans from $5,000 and up when that's what a business needs at a partic-ular time.)

MAKING FRIENDS WITH YOUR BANKER

"Many people think that when they apply for a loan the figures are fed into a computer that churns them up and spits out an an-swer. But the decision to make a loan is actually quite subjec-tive," says a banker. "If a banker is impressed with the prospec-tive borrower, then that person will get the money he needs. If the banker is not impressed, then he won't."

But what impresses bankers? And if it's not an evaluation of the figures, then why are they so essential?

These are important questions, and the bankers we asked assured us that bankers do, indeed, lend money based on their subjective assessments of borrowers' integrity and management savvy. Every banker we talked to agreed that the better the banker knows the small-business client, the better able to evalu-ate that entrepreneur's creditability that banker will be.

Yes, the figures are important, and not only for themselves. They are also important because bankers respect those men and women who are able and willing to put the figures together and to evaluate what they have to say about their businesses.

It makes sense that if your banker's decision will sub-stantially depend on your relationship with him or her, you would not want to wait until you need money before establishing your creditability. By then, it could be too late.

THE SEVEN Cs OF CREDITABILITY

Much of what your banker is looking for is described in the seven Cs of creditability:

1. *Character,* to a banker, means that borrowers keep their word. Borrowers who are honest and reliable, who will do everything they can to repay a loan, have character. It's a most important attribute. If a banker truly believes you are trustworthy and likes the way you present yourself and your business, your chances of getting a business loan increase.

2. *Capacity* demonstrates to a banker that the prospective borrower's financial strength and track record are sufficient to support loan payments. Bankers believe the past is probably a valid indication of the future. They prefer not to deal with those people who, despite long hours and great effort, seem to have problems keeping their businesses going. Bankers want borrowers who have demonstrated the capacity to meet their financial obligations.

3. *Community* involvement indicates to a banker that the borrower is committed to the business. The person who is involved in his or her local community has put down roots and will work hard for success. A person with deep community roots won't skip town without paying his or her debts.

4. *Capital* refers to the amount of equity an entrepreneur has in the company. Bankers want borrowers to have significant financial investments in their own businesses. There are three reasons why:
   - Equity provides a cushion in times of recession.
   - Personal investment shows that the owners believe in the value of the business as an investment.
   - Significant equity ensures that the owners would have too much to lose to close their doors if things get difficult.

5. *Collateral* is the property a borrower is willing to pledge to the bank as a secondary source of payment, should the first source (income and profits) dry up. An unsecured loan is one that is guaranteed only by the borrower's signature and has no attached collateral. Such a loan is a far greater risk to the bank and there would have to be an aspect of offsetting security in the borrower's character, capacity and capital before a banker would consider writing an unsecured loan.

6. *Conditions* include everything affecting a business that are outside of the borrower's control. For example, the banker may assess the degree to which a doubling in the price of paper in 1997 would affect the amount of business done by a small printer the following year, or how a prolonged drought would impact a small nursery, or whether the borrower's industry is being hit by foreign competition.

7. *Coverage* protects the banker in the event of disaster striking the business. Bankers want life insurance for the owner and fire and legal insurance for the business.

MEETING WITH YOUR BANKER

In order to establish your creditability you should make an appointment with your banker soon after you open your business account. Ask for time to review a copy of your business's most recent balance sheet and income (profit and loss) statement. (We'll explain how to prepare these reports in Chapter 9, "Presenting Your Bottom Line.")

It's quite possible that you will have to educate your banker about your industry as well as about your business. If, for instance, you own a bowling alley and newspapers are heralding a stay-at-home generation and predicting less money spent for outside entertainment, your banker will look to you for information on what your trade association is doing to keep bowling alleys appealing to their market niche.

During these early meetings, you should be assessing your banker's strengths and weaknesses as a business adviser. Remember, bankers see businesses with problems all the time. A good banker should be willing to give pertinent management advice when you run into problems, not just when you have borrowed and report that you can't make your payments. Bankers watch their own deposits; they are the first to know when the local business economy is expanding or contracting.

Entrepreneurs are optimistic, enthusiastic people and bankers wouldn't want them any other way. But as such, entrepreneurs seldom see all the risks. Because a good banker is trained to look for risk you can benefit by getting your banker's opinion (along with opinions from your CPA, attorney, and mentors) before you commit to extra staff or a new piece of equipment. Yes, the banker may be a cynic, but that will balance your resident optimist. If you involve your banker in the early planning stages she or he will not be taken by surprise when you come for financing.

TAKING A LONG-TERM VIEW

Obviously, by establishing an ongoing relationship with your banker you are letting go of the possibility of shopping for the best possible deal in return for the expectation of assistance in bad times as well as good. So don't undermine your efforts by going across the street just to get a quarter of a percent more for a certificate of deposit. You should use all the bank's services as often as possible—credit cards, safe deposit boxes, travelers' checks, notary public. Each use makes you a valued client, rather than another bank account number.

Possibly the most common way in which business owners undermine their value with bankers is by siphoning excess funds into money market accounts. Banks make their profits on the funds that are left with them, and if you deposit $100,000 in the morning and withdraw the same amount that afternoon, the banker only sees paperwork. Of course, it's good business to get the best return you can on your excess cash, but consider the bank's own short- and long-term certificates of deposit in order to keep your average balance reasonably high.

After George and Felicity Hunt had survived their Day of Disasters they consolidated their accounts at one bank, took in a set of financial documents, and applied for a line-of-credit in order to avoid such embarrassments in future.

"It was quick recovery time," says George. "I knew I'd been too casual with the first banker, so when the new banker said he'd look our figures over I asked him to stop by and look us over!"

"Two days later he just walked in," adds Felicity. "We had a crowd that night and he was obviously impressed. First thing the next morning he called to say we'd get our loan."

CHECKLIST: WHICH IS THE BEST BANK FOR YOUR BUSINESS? WHO IS THE BEST BANKER?

☐ What banks have convenient locations for my business?

☐ Which local banks best service small businesses?

☐ What banking services will my business need? Letters of credit, safe deposit box, payroll processing, secure overnight deposit, lines-of-credit, short- or long-term financing?

☐ What personal qualities in a banker would best complement my strengths and weaknesses and those of my key advisers?

☐ What recommendations for bankers have I heard? Whose opinion should I ask?

☐ Which bankers do I know personally? Whose reputation do I most respect? With whom do I have the best rapport?

☐ Do I have my seven Cs lined up? How will bankers evaluate me?

☐ How interested in servicing my business does this banker appear to be?

☐ Is the lending authority of this banker within the range of the credit I might need?

☐ Does my first-choice banker seem flexible and willing to discuss the needs of my business?

☐ How well does my banker know me and my business?

☐ How do the strengths and weaknesses of my banker fit with the strengths and weaknesses of my key advisers?

☐ How can I make better use of my banker's knowledge of small-business finances and the money marketplace?

☐ Which bank services can I use to ensure that my banker values both my personal and my business banking?

5

Getting the Bank on Your Side

Borrowing money is tough and getting tougher. Whether you're starting a business or expanding into a new market, getting a loan in the 1990s is far more difficult than it was in the 1980s, particularly for small businesses. Bankers are making greater demands of their entrepreneurial clients than ever before.

FOUR BANKING DEMANDS ENTREPRENEURS MUST MEET

1. **Small-business owners pay higher rates than large corporations.** Big businesses still have the clout to negotiate interest rates that are close to prime, but small businesses are asked to pay from two to five points more. If money is tight—nationally, in your state, or locally—you'll be offered a higher interest rate than when money is easy to get—if you can get a loan at all. A track record of having paid off a prior loan consistently and on time will always be a point in your favor.

2. **Bankers are demanding more financial statements.** Bankers have always wanted entrepreneurs to prove the income source that will pay off the loan, and now they are demanding that this source be more certain or be backed up by a second or third source of income in case the first source fails. This is really to your advantage. Because businesses have to be leaner as we approach the twenty-first century, the extra steps your banker demands will help you to avoid taking unrealistic risks.

3. **More collateral is being required than ever before.** Some bankers are asking for collateral worth three or more times the amount of the loans, claiming that the equipment being financed will depreciate and not be worth as much if and when they have to claim it. Really, they are stacking the odds against their ever having to seize any collateral. Some banks are insisting that home equity be used to collateralize startup business loans. Frankly, you are better off using two pieces of equipment as collateral on a loan than using your home, even though the latter may be easier to arrange. Should the economy plummet and your business go under despite your every effort, you're better off with your home than with your equipment.

4. **Small businesses need to show a greater ratio of assets to debts than they did a decade ago.** Nowadays bankers want entrepreneurs to have three to five times as much equity in their businesses as they are carrying in loans. In the 1980s, twice as much equity to debt (a ratio of 2:1) would have been sufficient. This is one of those areas where bankers can be flexible. The better your banker trusts your integrity and your management skills, and the less trendy or risky your business or product is, the more likely he or she is to be satisfied with a lower asset-to-debt ratio.

The fact is, some small-business owners whose borrowing power was good in the 1980s lost their creditability completely in the 1990s, for a couple of reasons:

■ Bankers have become much more wary of businesses that are based on trends. In the 1980s there was an attitude that a good trend would never end, but now we admit that's not true.

- Then there was the savings and loan industry crisis, which resulted in federal examiners urging commercial bankers to be much more cautious. All bankers got the message that they could be held embarrassingly accountable for bad loans.

"Bankers don't want to make mistakes," says banking consultant Roger Bel Air. "Since the charge-off rate of bad loans for a bank is only 1.5 percent, bankers need to be at least 98.5 percent sure the money is going to be repaid."

CHECK YOUR CREDIT

Before asking for a loan, before meeting with a new banker, before you even shop for a new bank, check your credit rating.

If you already have a banker, call and ask which credit bureaus the bank uses; otherwise, write or call all of them and arrange to get a report on your credit. The fee will be nominal.

Do this, no matter how clean you think your record is. There may have been late fees on one of your charge accounts because of computer errors—which may even have been reversed—and they may show up on your credit report. Or you may have been billed for goods that were returned and the skirmish settled months ago; the charges may still show up on your credit report. If you see anything on your credit report that you believe is incorrect, you have the right to file a statement that must be released to anybody receiving a copy of the report.

If anything on your credit report is to your discredit, tell your banker that it is there, explain the situation as best you can, and assure your banker that it isn't going to happen again. At the least, you'll get points for your honesty.

BANKERS AVOID MINDSETS

One of the evaluations bankers make about their clients is the stability of their mindsets. Your "mindset" to these bankers is the way you see your business.

- Entrepreneurs with **sales mindsets** tend to believe that if they do a good job selling their product everything else will take care of itself. When things are not going well, they tend to concentrate on increasing sales.

- People with **production mindsets** are those who come from a technical background. They believe that all their problems will take care of themselves if the product or service is absolutely top quality. When things are not going well, they tend to concentrate on quality control and higher productivity.

- Business owners with a **management mindset** usually have a mid-level corporate background, and they think all the problems will be taken care of if the operation is well organized and the staff well trained. When things are not going well they tend to concentrate on organization and staff problems.

- You could say that bankers have a **financial mindset,** in that they believe that when things go wrong the entrepreneur should concentrate on the figures.

Obviously, you must know your production side, because in today's market it takes a quality product to succeed. You must also know how to market your product or service, because the competition is fierce. And if you haven't effectively organized your business, that is, your time and your employees' time, the product won't be produced efficiently or shipped expeditiously when it is sold. Finally, if you ignore your financials, you won't know whether, or why, your costs are escalating or your profits are dropping.

Savvy bankers seek small-business owners who look at all four areas to see where the problem is, and who concentrate their remedial efforts wherever they are needed. These entrepreneurs frequently have that rare quality of being excruciatingly honest with themselves. And if they have a preconceived expectation, it's that problems will most often arise in the areas where they are weakest.

Good bankers know that looking at your business from a single perspective or mindset, rather than with an integrated management viewpoint, is likely to leave you in need of money and unable to get it. One banker described such a would-be borrower, saying, "They have an excellent product, a well-trained staff, and satisfied customers. But they have absolutely no idea why they ran out of money, or even how much they need. When I ask for financial statements they tell me about the large contract they are on the brink of signing!

"And what they really don't understand is that if they have their accountant put the financial statements together overnight and bring them into my office tomorrow, I'm still not going to make them a loan. I want lead time. I don't make loans to people who come in at their eleventh hour. I want to know *that they know* what their financials are telling us."

THE FIVE MOST COMMON REASONS WHY BANKERS REFUSE TO MAKE LOANS

1. The owner's equity is too low in relation to the amount of the loan. Bankers want to see that you have too much to lose to walk away if the business is failing.
2. There is no secondary source of repayment, or the value of the collateral offered is too low or seems unreliable.
3. The business is a one-person enterprise, with no backup staff if the owner is suddenly incapacitated.
4. The banker believes that the product or service is sound but the projections are weak and that the business will need longer than the bank's usual term to repay the loan.
5. The banker thinks the applicant has inadequate managerial experience or ability.

"I actually see people tremble when they come in to ask for a loan," says a banker. "To me the request is business as usual, and that's what it needs to be to my client. It really has no more emotional content than if we were negotiating a wheat purchase. If you were buying wheat from me all you'd think about is the price and terms; you certainly wouldn't be worried about personal rejection. Yet when small-business owners ask me for a loan—and my commodity is lending money—for which they are willing to pay a fee called interest, this 'maybe I'm not worthy' fear gets activated. Entrepreneurs have to realize that when their loans are rejected there's a reason, and it's not personal, it's business."

Translation: Ask the banker why your application has been rejected, and what would have to be changed to make it acceptable.

WAYS TO APPROACH A BANKER SUCCESSFULLY

Conduct yourself in a thoughtful, professional manner when approaching a banker by making note of the suggestions that follow.

Be Professional

Would you visit your doctor without an appointment? Would you visit your best client without an appointment? Of course not. Yet every day people walk into banks, walk up to the manager, ask for a loan, and wonder why they hear, "The bank is not lending at this time." When you need to talk with your banker, call and make an appointment. Bankers are organized, they appreciate courtesy, and they don't make loans to strangers. You wouldn't walk in on your accountant, or your attorney, so when you want to see your banker, arrange an appointment.

Make Your Banker Your Partner

Entrepreneurs automatically try to convince their bankers with their own enthusiasm; but enthusiasm alone won't get you a loan.

When you sit down with your banker, you need to say, "This is the situation, these are the challenges, and these are the opportunities facing us. This is how I propose to proceed. What do you think?" In other words, you must identify and reveal both the positive and the negative aspects of the situation facing your company, and then involve your banker in a discussion of how you can capitalize on the positive and minimize the negative.

Be prepared for questions about your company's strengths and weaknesses. The strengths are what you want your banker to appreciate; the weaknesses add credibility and give you an opportunity to explain your next moves.

This approach demonstrates your ability to manage your business, to see the situation clearly and take the necessary steps to meet your long-term objectives. It's an approach that can respond in a considered way to obstacles, even unexpectedly sudden obstacles, and it's an approach that can take advantage of new opportunities without seeming to go in a new direction every time the sun rises. Apart from demonstrating your banking savvy, this approach gives your banker insights into you and your business.

Suppose you visit your banker because you need to upgrade a piece of machinery in order to get enough volume to handle a large order that, if successfully met, could become a standing monthly order. Your banker could help you to assess the financial viability of some alternatives, such as paying your staff to work double shifts, buying the new equipment, leasing it, or renting time on a competitor's machine.

Your banker's ability to see alternatives comes from dealing with a multitude of small businesses and realizing that their problems are infinite variations on a few central issues. In addition, your banker undoubtedly has a better reading on the local economy than the average business owner could possibly have. You know when your own sales are rising or falling, but your banker will have that information for the entire town and all the businesses in it.

Consulting your banker gives him or her the opportunity to respond as a partner and make suggestions that will help you to fine-tune your business plan. You are assuring him or her that you welcome early input then, and again if and when things don't go as expected. When you take this approach, you make it possible to consult with your banker about altering the terms of your loan if your sales should drop unexpectedly or if there is another, unexpected, drain on your cash.

"My whole attention is in my town, not in San Francisco or Los Angeles," says a banker in a small California town. "I'm out in the community and can see what's going on and what's not, so the main office puts their trust in my decisions down here. Whenever a small-business person comes in, it's usually someone trying to run a business by herself and needing an adviser. A banker, a good banker, is the cheapest adviser you can get. I don't know anything about running a candy store, or small manufacturing, but I know what's happening in this area and I can analyze figures."

By treating your banker as a partner and dealing honestly with your partner, you are establishing your creditability—which is what your banker is really seeking.

Promote Your Banker

Have you ever thought about how bankers rise in the banking hierarchy? They do so by making money, and there are *three* ways you can help them to make money.

When you have a good relationship with your banker, you make it easier for her or him to lend you money. When you consult your banker before the need for money is crucial, you make it possible for her or him to advise you on how to make your request impossible to turn down. When your banker makes you a loan, you both win.

You can also make money for your banker by becoming a full-service customer and by using the full range of services that her or his bank offers.

Finally, you can recommend your banker when your chamber or trade association needs a speaker, when your daughter needs a car loan, and (most valuable of all) when a new entrepreneur asks for a recommendation. Bankers are like elephants—they don't forget.

CHECKLIST: PRELIMINARY BUSINESS PLAN QUESTIONS

☐ Have I checked my credit record, and done anything necessary to correct it?

☐ Do I usually solve problems from a sales viewpoint, a production orientation, a management perspective, or a financial mindset? Which is my strength and which is my weakness?

☐ How will this business be organized: sole proprietorship, partnership, corporation? How many owners will there be and what functions will they fill?

☐ What kind of business is it? Construction, manufacturing, distribution, retail, service, export, transportation?

☐ What is the best way to describe my product or service?

☐ Are there local zoning requirements the business must meet? How will this be done?

☐ What licenses will the business need and where and how are they obtained?

☐ Where will the business be located? What are the advantages and disadvantages of this location?

☐ If we are leasing space, who from and what are the terms of the lease?

☐ What kinds of insurance does the business need? How will we meet these needs? How much will our insurance cost?

☐ What financial records will be kept and who will keep them?

☐ What will the overhead costs be per month and per year?

☐ How will the price of the product or service be determined?

☐ How much competition will the business have? What kind of competition?

☐ Who will the customers be? Where will they come from?

☐ How will we advertise or promote the product or service? What is the estimated cost of advertising and promotion per month and per year?

☐ Who will supply the business? Which of these will be good credit references?

- ☐ How many people will be employed? How many immediately, within six months, within a year?
- ☐ Where and how will we find employees?
- ☐ What will the payroll be over the next six months, the next twelve months?
- ☐ What are my plans for future growth?
- ☐ How much capital do I have and what will be invested in the business?
- ☐ How much capital will I need over the next year, three years, six years? How will I raise this capital?

6

All Loans
Are Not Created
Equal

Many small-business owners start out with high hopes for their businesses and never suspect that there will be periods of negative cash flow. Yet, for most entrepreneurs borrowing eventually becomes a fact of business life.

At this point you could find yourself having to learn a new language.

LA LINGUA BANCA

Bankers group loans under several different headings, such as business cycle loans, working capital loans and fixed asset loans. Then, to make things really confusing, bankers have a number of different ways of designing the loans under each heading. For instance, business cycle loans can be issued as either lines-of-credit or short-term loans, while expansion loans can be written as interim loans, long-term loans, or second mortgages. The problem, or challenge, is that when you go to your banker to borrow funds for your business, you will be asked what sort of loan you need from the first group described and then offered a loan from the second group.

The difficulty, or opportunity, is compounded by your need to decide if the proffered loan is the most cost-effective way to meet your needs. It's no wonder surveys show that borrowers feel they are at a great disadvantage when they go to bankers. Not only do the bankers control the money that borrowers need, the bankers are the only ones who know what they are talking about!

So let's cut through the technical jargon and identify what you must ask for to meet your needs and what you can anticipate from your banker in return.

HOW LOANS ARE PACKAGED

Working Capital Loans

Working capital is the amount tied up in current assets (such as inventory and receivables) and on hand for current expenses. Every business should know how many months worth of current expenses it is prudent to have on hand and how this amount varies for them throughout the year. Having cash reserves to cover the expenses of at least three months is a good starting place.

A working capital loan is needed when something happens that causes the cash reserve needed for day-to-day expenses to be increased. This could occur if receivables are stretching, additional staff is hired, or inventory is increased.

A banker will want to know why you need this additional working capital. If the cause is additional staff or increased inventory, the banker will want to be shown how these added expenses will result in increased profits from which the loan can be repaid. If it is taking longer for you to collect your receivables due, the banker will want assurance that the receivables are not becoming uncollectible, that there are other funds to pay off the loan, and that steps are being taken to speed collections.

Working capital loans may be written with interest-only payments until the note (loan) is due, but are more often written with monthly payments of both principal and interest. The best package will have minimum monthly payments to cover the interest due on the amount you have drawn and will allow you to make payments of any size, and at any time, against the principal.

Business Cycle Loans

Any company that does most of its business at specific times of the year has seasonal business cycles. A gift store, for instance, that does most of its business before Christmas and in the summer tourism season has two cycles a year. A business cycle loan is expected to generate increased sales during a specific period. Bankers call this period of increased sales the time of asset conversion. Bankers usually categorize business cycle loans as low risk, because they expect to be paid from the increased sales within a short period of time.

There are several ways to meet business cycle credit needs. One is to negotiate an extended payment period with suppliers. Another is to obtain a bank loan on which interest is paid each month, with a single payment of principal at a specified time corresponding with the peak of the selling period.

Fixed-Asset Loans

Fixed assets are the business purchases that are not rolled over into cash as part of the business operations. Fixed-asset loans are usually written with monthly or quarterly payments of both principal and interest. The length of the loan is correlated to the expectation for increased profit, and the equipment purchased is pledged as collateral. Bankers consider the loans relatively risky, because so many factors can affect your expectations. Fixed-assets loans fall into three categories.

1. Safest from a banker's perspective is equipment and machinery that will be used to generate income. Bankers prefer to finance machinery and equipment that results in lower costs or more units produced.

2. Bankers are more cautious about fixed-asset borrowing for equipment or leasehold improvements that won't directly gen-

erate income, but will make working conditions easier or improve your image with clients. For such a loan, you will need to show that your current profits justify the expense.

3. The riskiest fixed-asset loan in a banker's eyes is one that is used to expand facilities. In this situation, bankers expect to see a corresponding increase in working capital to make use of the enlarged facilities. The fixed asset portion of the loan would be written to be paid off from the long-term profits resulting from the expansion.

Product Development Loans

Unless the development of a new product is in its later stages, where a prototype has been test marketed, most bankers consider these loans too risky to make. While product development is usually financed by investment equity, a bank loan may be arranged if the company can show a history of developing new products and can show that current profits are sufficient to pay off the loan even if the new product does not materialize. On these loans, bankers will usually want monthly principal and interest payments and will probably require collateral.

Real Estate Loans

When your business is ready to move into its own facility, a realty or property loan—equivalent to a home mortgage—may be arranged by your banker. Just as an individual has to qualify for a home mortgage by having sufficient income, your business will have to generate sufficient profits to meet the loan payments. Depending on the company's assets, a loan may be granted that will cover the purchase of the new facility and any renovation needed before you can relocate your company.

THE LOAN YOU GET

When you make an appointment to discuss a loan, your banker will expect you to have a specific reason why you need to borrow money. She or he will want to know how the need arose, what you could have done to anticipate it, and how the funds will be spent. You can make points with your banker by setting up a meeting to discuss the loan when you first anticipate an eventual need for additional funds—well before you need the money. Bankers like that situation.

Your banker then expects your financial statements to justify the amount you ask for and will question whether that amount is either too high or too low. However, banks seldom negotiate the amount of the loan, even though they are aware that lending too little can be as risky as lending too much. Instead they will assess your request and refuse to write the loan if they think you have asked for the wrong amount. This is one reason why it is so important to discuss your financing needs with your banker while they are still in the future; that way, you will have a good idea of how much your banker thinks you need. Presumably if you then ask for a different amount you will also be prepared to justify your request with the sorts of figures and facts your banker will respect.

HOW LONG WILL YOUR LOAN BE FOR?

When you approach your banker for a working capital, business cycle, fixed-asset, product development, or realty loan, you should not only know what to ask for, you should have thought about the type of payments that would best suit your business and the current situation. The longer the term (life) of the loan, the more likely it is that the banker will want regular payments of both principal and interest. However, if you can show a predictable and fairly certain increase in profits by a specific date, you may be able to obtain a loan on which you make interest payments until that date and then pay off the loan with a "balloon" payment.

The term (length) of the loan should relate to your reason for seeking additional financing. For instance, a loan to build your retail inventory by 20 percent before the ski season should generate increased sales as soon as snow falls, certainly within a matter of months; whereas a new piece of equipment for a new product line might generate far more income over a longer period, but not until the product is launched and finds its market niche.

Bankers use several criteria in determining the length for which a loan should be written:

- They evaluate the way the loan is to be used and when the purpose of the loan (i.e., inventory, wages) will be converted into cash (i.e., sales, services).

- They evaluate the life expectancy of any fixed assets to be purchased with the funds, and they expect that equipment to work productively for longer than the life of the loan.

- They endeavor to select a loan term that logically relates to the amount of time needed to generate the profits to pay off the loan.

- They have their own internal "term:risk" ratios that dictate the maximum periods for specific amounts and purposes. For instance, one bank might limit inventory loans of $15,000 or less to 90 days, another might write such loans for a maximum of 180 days. Or a bank might limit its small equipment loans to three to five years, but write the same loans with an SBA guarantee for five to seven years because the SBA's participation reduces the bank's risk.

Understanding what criteria bankers use is the first step in negotiating the best loan you can get.

CHECKLIST: CAN YOU SPEAK THE LANGUAGE?

Define the following terms so that you are sure you know how they differ. Which do banks write? Which might you need?

☐ Business cycle loans

_____

_____

☐ Working capital loans

_____

_____

☐ Fixed-asset loans

_____

_____

☐ Line-of-credit loans

_____

_____

☐ Short-term loan

_____

_____

☐ Product development loans

_____

_____

☐ Property loans

_____

_____

☐ Long-term loans

_____

_____

☐ Time of asset conversion

_____

_____

7

A Loan by Any Other Name

Just sitting down with a banker and asking for a loan can result in an extreme state of confusion for many entrepreneurs. A small-business owner may know enough to ask for a working capital loan, rather than asking for "money until our sales pick up." But then the entrepreneur might be offered a line-of-credit loan, a term loan, an installment loan, a commercial loan, or our bank's special loan."

This wouldn't be such a problem if these were all different names for the same type of loan, but regrettably they are not. The confusion results from the lack of standard terminology in the banking industry. For instance, a commercial loan might be a line-of-credit at one bank and a term loan at another bank. And a term loan might be written with equal installments of principal and interest at one bank, while at the bank across the street a term loan might be written with monthly interest payments and a balloon payment of the principal.

In Chapter 6, "All Loans Are Not Created Equal," we described the types of loans small-business owners might be offered under names that bankers recognize. In this chapter we will describe how banks structure those same loans and explain their common variations. With this information you will be armed with the facts necessary to understand just what your banker is offering you.

LINES-OF-CREDIT

The most useful type of loan for any business is the line-of-credit. In fact, it's probably the one permanent loan arrangement every entrepreneur should have with his or her banker. Lines-of-credit give you access to cash when you need emergency funds, when you have the opportunity to purchase supplies at a volume cash discount, or when your cash flow has slowed to a trickle for reasons outside your control.

A line-of-credit is a short-term loan (usually written for a maximum of one year) that extends the cash available in your business's checking account to the upper limit of the loan contract. Every bank has its own method of funding lines-of-credit, but usually the credit line is not activated until the business's checking account is depleted, and then amounts equal to the checks to be covered are automatically transferred into the business's checking account as those checks are deposited. A common variation occurs if the bank has a minimum amount that can be transferred on any one day. Increasingly, bankers want to be notified with a phone call when you write a check that will draw on the credit line.

The business pays interest on the actual amount advanced from the time it is advanced until it is paid back. Unsecured lines-of-credit are only written in low-risk situations, and usually carry the bank's lowest interest rate. Credit lines secured by receivables or inventory carry higher interest rates, justified by the expense to the bank of having to monitor the collateral. If possible, avoid a bank that includes a clause in its contract that gives it the right to cancel the loan if the bank perceives that your business is in jeopardy. Another possible clause might escalate the rate of interest if the bank feels the loan has become too risky.

Even if your loan only requires that the interest be paid each month, it's wise to make payments on the principal as frequently as you are able. Bankers prefer that the monies not sit in your account, but that you use the loan as a revolving credit line. Paying down the principal regularly indicates to the bank that your business is earning the income to justify such a loan.

Many lines-of-credit are written for terms (periods) of one year and may be renewed almost automatically for an annual fee. Some banks require that the credit line be fully paid off for between a week and a month of the end of each contract year. This period may be the best time to negotiate for a better rate of interest or any other changes you want.

There are some restrictions on how you can use lines-of-credit. The loans are intended for working capital and business cycle needs—in other words, for purchases of inventory and payment of operating costs. They are not intended for the purchase of equipment or machinery, and certainly not for real estate. However, they are intended for emergency coverage, which means that if a piece of expensive machinery has a major breakdown and must be replaced within a day, you would be justified in using your credit line. But in this type of situation you should immediately arrange with your banker for an equipment loan. Otherwise you would be violating your line-of-credit contract, and it could be canceled.

Even if you don't need a line-of-credit now, talk to your banker about how to get one. Bankers don't like writing any type of loan in an emergency, especially one they only give to businesses that are financially sound. So credit lines must be set up as "normal operating procedure." To negotiate a credit line, your banker will want to see current financial statements, the latest tax returns, and a projected cash-flow statement. (We fully describe these statements in the next chapters.)

INSTALLMENT LOANS

These loans are paid back with equal monthly payments covering both principal and interest. Installment loans may be written to meet any of the loan requirements described in Chapter 6. With these types of loans, you receive the full amount of the loan when the contract is signed, and interest is calculated from that day to the final day of the loan. Installment loans should not carry prepayment penalties, and the interest should be adjusted if the loan is paid off early.

The term of an installment loan is always related to its use. A business cycle installment loan might be for as little as three or four months, an equipment installment loan might be for one to seven years, while real estate and renovation loans may be written for up to twenty-one years. Generally, the shorter the term of the loan, the lower the interest rate will be, since banks assume that shorter loans expose them to less risk.

Installment loans are sometimes written with quarterly, half-yearly, or annual payments. It would be appropriate to ask for such an arrangement if the loan is to finance a project that will generate income at quarterly, half-yearly, or annual intervals. These arrangements are also called "balloon" payments.

BALLOON LOANS

Although balloon loans are generally written under a different name, they can be identified by their payment schedules. With balloon loans, the full amount is received when the contract is signed, but only the interest is paid off during the life of the loan (usually with monthly payments), and a "balloon" payment of the full amount of the principal becomes due on the final day. Occasionally a banker will offer a loan in which payments are for interest and some principal, or where both interest and principal are paid with a single "balloon" (final) payment.

Balloon loans are usually reserved for situations when a business has to wait until a specific date before receiving payments from a client for its product or services. In all other ways they are the same as installment loans.

Sometimes a first or second mortgage is offered in balloon format, even though the business borrowing the funds does not expect a specific income amount that will pay off the loan coincidentally with its maturation. The intention with such loans is that another mortgage will be written when the balloon loan matures, and the risk to the borrower in this situation is much higher than the risk a bank would expose itself to. The borrower has no guarantee that banks will be writing loans during the period when the balloon loan expires, nor that any loans being written will be reasonably priced. More than one entrepreneur has relied on an oral promise by a banker that there "will be no problem writing a follow-up loan," only to find that this was not the case when the next loan was needed.

SECURED AND UNSECURED LOANS

When your banker knows you well and is convinced that your business is sound and that the loan will be repaid on time, he or she may be willing to write an unsecured loan. Such a loan, in any of the forms we have described, has no collateral pledged as a secondary payment source should you default. Banks write unsecured loans only with people whom they consider to be no- or low-risk. Secured loans, on the other hand, require some type of collateral, and because they are still perceived as being more risky, they generally carry interest rates that are equal to or higher than the rate that would be given on similar unsecured loans.

Bankers routinely ask for collateral when a loan is being written for more than twelve months or is for the purchase of equipment. The collateral used, whether equipment, inventory, or real estate, is expected to outlast the loan. Plus, the collateral is usually related to the purpose of the loan, except when a banker insists that a loan be secured by home equity. As bankers expect the collateral to pay off the loan if the borrower defaults, they will value that collateral appropriately. Therefore, a $40,000 piece of new equipment will probably secure a loan of only $30,000.

EIGHT LOAN VARIATIONS

Banks all over the country write loans, especially installment and balloon loans, under a wide variety of names. They include:

- Term loans, both short- and long-term according to the number of years for which they are written.

- Equity loans or second mortgages, where real estate is used to secure a loan. These are usually long-term.

- Accounts receivable loans, which are secured by your outstanding accounts and may be written for up to 75 percent of the value of those accounts.

- Inventory loans for the purchase of inventory and, if secured by that inventory, limited to up to 50 percent of its sale price.

- Equipment loans for the purchase of, and secured by, new equipment.

- Guaranteed loans in which a third party—an investor, spouse, or even the SBA—guarantees repayment.

- Commercial loans in which the bank offers its usual business loan.

- Personal loans in which your signature and personal collateral guarantee the loan, which you in turn lend to the business. In fact, if yours is a small proprietorship or wholly owned corporation, any loan your business makes will undoubtedly require your personal guarantee of repayment.

EARLY OR NOT AT ALL

It's important to remember that bankers don't like lending to people, or businesses, who are in need. Nor do they like to be the sole financiers. Whether you are buying inventory for the tourism season or a new printing press, your banker will expect you to finance part of the expense yourself and to minimize the bank's risk. Probably the single best move you can make for your business's financial future is to see your banker early, demonstrate an understanding of your financials, and *discuss the loan you may need in the future, before the future is here.*

CHECKLIST: HOW WELL DO YOU KNOW LOAN DEFINITIONS?

☐ Which loans are commonly written with interest-only month-ly payments?

_____

_____

☐ How long is a short-term loan?

_____

_____

☐ Which loans revolve?

_____

_____

☐ Which has the lower interest rate, a secured or an unsecured loan? What are the two reasons?

_____

_____

☐ Name four types of collateral for business loans?

_____

_____

☐ Who may guarantee a loan? What does that mean?

_____

_____

☐ Which loan is the most desirable for every business to have?

_____

_____

☐ Why are balloon loans risky for the borrower?

_____

_____

8

The Perfect
Loan Application

Choosing the right bank and establishing a good relationship with a banker is like selecting the right market niche for your product and courting your potential buyers with your professional image and great service. Getting a loan is like writing the customer's order, and your loan application package is your sales tool.

When this sales tool combines the right mixture of facts and figures, it will sell your banker on the short- and long-term profit potential of lending money to your business. To do this, the loan application package must convince your banker that you will pay back the loan as promised and that your business's profitability and its future borrowing needs will result in a profit-making partnership.

For the most part, your loan application package has to do most of its selling without your presence. True, you will be there to explain the projections and justify the conclusions when you first present the application; but if the amount you need exceeds the lending authority of your banker, the loan application package will have to sell itself as it rises through the organization to the bank officer with the proper lending authority.

AN EFFECTIVE LOAN APPLICATION PACKAGE

First, a good loan application package is a financial portrait of your business in the form of a businesslike set of documents. As such, it should be filled with facts, not fantasies. For example, if you are describing your business, the statement "Classic Computers has grown faster than any other computer company in the county" would bring out the skepticism in most bankers. But if you write, "Classic Computers repairs clients' computers in their offices or provides them with a replacement computer within an hour. This service has built customer loyalty so that our repeat business has doubled each year for the past five years," you will surely impress your banker.

Next, the forecast statements in the loan application package should walk the fine line of realistic optimism. For example, if you predict an increase in sales of between 10 and 15 percent, you should base your income projection figures on an increase of 10 or 12 percent, and then describe the steps you will take and the reasons you think you will achieve a 15 percent increase.

Finally, the application must be complete. When a section of a loan application package is missing, bankers instantly suspect that either something is being hidden or the applicant doesn't know his or her business well enough to obtain and present all the necessary information.

THE CONTENTS OF A LOAN APPLICATION PACKAGE

1. Cover sheet
2. Cover letter
3. Table of contents
4. Statement of amount and use of the loan
5. History and description of the business
6. Functions and background of the management team
7. Market information on the product or service

8. Financial history and current status
9. Financial projections
10. List of potential collateral
11. Personal financial statements
12. Additional documents to support the application

THE LOAN APPLICATION PACKAGE EXPLAINED

Each element of the loan application package has its own particular requirements.

Cover Sheet

The title page of your package includes specific information:

Loan Application
Submitted by Sally Forth, Soxsessful Hose
To Sugar Daddy Bank, Main Street, Coppertown.

Submitted on (current date)

By

Ms. Sally Forth
Soxsessful Hose
123 Main St.
Coppertown
(100) 111-1234
(fax) 111-1235

Cover Letter

The cover letter is a business letter addressed to your banker. In the first paragraph, you request his or her consideration of your application for either a line-of-credit or installment loan.

In the second paragraph, describe your business: "Our company is a (sole proprietorship, partnership, corporation), in (manufacturing, retailing, distributing) of (whatever type of goods or services)."

In the third paragraph, take the opportunity to sell your application by describing, briefly, your future plans.

If you prefer to be really formal, call this page an executive summary, and leave out the salutation.

Table of Contents

Include this page to make it easy for your banker to see that all the necessary documents are included.

Statement of Amount and Use of the Loan

This page gives you the opportunity to make the case for your loan. Start by stating how much you require and the purpose it will be put to; then expand and justify your reasons for needing the cash.

If you are seeking a loan for more than one purpose, divide your request into long-term, mid-term, and short-term purposes, such as equity in facilities, short-term fixed assets, and working capital.

If you are buying a new piece of equipment, begin by listing the contract price; add the cost of freight, installation, and taxes; deduct the amount you will be contributing; then show the balance to be borrowed. Follow that by describing the equipment in terms of its function: What will it do? How will that make or save money for the business? Will it be used for current orders or to enable a new line of business? How long will it take for its production or cost-saving attributes to equal its cost of purchase?

If you are requesting money to build inventory or to cover overhead, describe the need and justify it in a similar manner. In other words, focus on the profitability of the business either by increased production or decreased expenses, and include short- and long-term results. Keep these statements simple and brief; you will be using the financial projections to spell out the figures that justify these statements.

If all or part of the equity contribution toward these new expenses is coming from other people, you should say whether this capital is in the form of an equity loan or an investment, and what payback or buyout is planned. An "equity loan" means that all parties will treat these monies as investment funds until such time as the business is able to pay them back. Equity loans can carry interest, but as the payment is deferred until all regular loans are repaid, they can be treated as equity, or ownership, investment. A banker won't want to see a regular loan from another source used as your equity contribution to new financing, but an equity loan is usually acceptable.

History and Description of Your Business

For many small-business owners, these are the most difficult one-to-three pages to write. There are two keys to success:

1. Stay with the facts.
2. Assume the reader knows nothing about your business.

Begin with the company's history: when it started and (listed by date) each significant step of its growth. Next, provide more information on the legal form of your business, and then expand on its location.

Finally, explain your industry and your product as briefly and simply as possible. Go into as much detail as you would if your favorite aunt were to ask, "But why Soxsessful Hose anyway, dear? How do you know what people want? And why would they go to a specialty store to buy nylons?"

Highlight Your Management Team

Bankers know that it's people who make things happen, and your team of employees, mentors and consultants are the people who will make your business happen under your leadership. Keep this section to just one or two pages, and list people by name as you describe their responsibilities.

Start with the leader, yourself (this is easier to write in third person), and describe those skills and knowledge that make you the right person to be running this business.

Next describe each of your employees, or groups of employees, in the same terms. Include enough on each person's background to show that he or she is the best person to handle this important part of your operations.

Be sure to say who is in control when you are away. Bankers are known for turning down applications that rely too heavily on a few key people, so you want to show that your staff is capable of running the business even when a key person is absent.

Although your mentors and consultants (such as a friend with a similar retail business in another town, your accountant, and your attorney) are not on your staff, name them in your loan application package and describe their ongoing contributions to the business.

Market Information on Your Product or Service

Four items must be covered on these pages, and each should be fully described. Take as much space as is really necessary to cover the current and near-future situation.

1. Describe your product line or service and the market it serves.
2. Describe how you have targeted this market niche, and evaluate how successful your marketing has been.
3. In specific steps, describe your plans to improve your marketing in the future.
4. Describe how you intend to develop your current product line or service and/or add additional products and services.

Your descriptions should demonstrate a thorough understanding of who your customers are (their age, location, gender, lifestyle, purchasing power, etc.) and why they are attracted to your product, as well as your awareness of your competitors' strengths and weaknesses, the advantages you have over your competitors, and your plans for overcoming your own disadvantages. Be specific.

Financial History and Current Status

Your banker will want to see your balance sheets and income (profit-and-loss) statements (we'll go into them in the next chapter), as well as tax returns for the previous three to five years. But financial statements alone don't mean very much. To extract their value, bankers compare this year's figures to those of previous years, looking for trends and significant changes. Through these comparisons, they glean information that reveals the profitability of your products, your ability to manage costs, and how your business is developing compared to the norms of your industry.

Startups with only a current balance sheet and income statement (each of which will probably cover less than a year) can overcome some of their disadvantages by providing either quarterly or monthly statements.

Financial Projections

This set of three documents must be cast to show how the business, with the use of the loan, will generate the profits necessary to pay back the bank. They include the following items:

1. A projected income statement
2. A projected balance sheet
3. A projected cash budget

Projected (also called pro forma) financials are prepared from this year's figures using established trends and industry information to forecast the future. A sample of a projected cash flow budget is presented in Chapter 9, "Presenting Your Bottom Line."

If you do not have forecasting (spreadsheet) software, your accountant can prepare these for you. However, you must ensure that he or she has information on any major changes you are planning, and you should review the completed documents in order to answer your banker's questions.

> **Tip** Draw on your accountant's expertise. Your accountant will be your most valuable adviser in preparing your loan application package, and not only with the financial statements and financial projections.

List of Potential Collateral

Listing your available collateral serves two purposes. First, it demonstrates your understanding that your banker will look for a backup source of repayment. Second, it may demonstrate to your banker that you have sufficient assets to be classed as a low-risk borrower and be offered an unsecured loan.

Potential collateral includes cash reserves, stocks and bonds, equipment, home equity, inventory, and receivables. Bankers have clear preferences for certain types of collateral. (They tend to put the highest value on home equity both for its surest conversion to cash and because it is the asset you are least likely to abandon.)

Each piece of collateral listed should be fully identified and, where appropriate, described with its cost and current fair market value. Only the "free" value of any equipment or property can be used as collateral for a loan, the "free" part being that portion of the value that is not currently mortgaged.

The **list of potential collateral** can be shown as part of a **schedule of term debts** (see the chart titled "List of Potential Assets"). In such a schedule, you would first list those assets that are fully paid for with their various values, then list those assets that carry loans from shortest to longest maturity.

CHART OF POTENTIAL ASSETS

Equipment Description	Purchase Price	Purchase Date	Life Expectancy	Depreciated Value	Fair Market Value	Loan Held by	Years to Maturity	Current Debt	Free Equity
A.	B.	C.	D.	E.	F.	G.	H.	I.	J.

A. Describe each item well enough to be identified. Include brand, model and serial numbers, size, color, etc.

B. & C. Refer to purchase documentation, which your banker may wish to see on those items used as collateral.

D. Documented life expectancy is preferred to estimates, but put something.

E. See your tax files or accountant for depreciated value.

F. Manufacturers frequently have information on resale prices for major pieces of equipment. Or look for a reasonable estimate in trade newspapers or magazines.

G. "No" or give the name of the loan holder.

H. Calculate the months or years until the loan will be fully paid.

I. The remaining balance should be available from the lender.

J. Free equity is the fair market value of the equipment if there is no loan, less the current debt if there is a loan.

Personal Financial Statements

Unless your business is extremely solid financially, you will most likely be asked to add your personal guarantee to any loan the bank makes. Therefore, the banker will also want to see your (each owner's) most recent tax return and balance sheets showing personal net worth. Most banks have preprinted forms that make gathering and presenting these figures relatively easy.

Additional Documents

In this section you can include any documents you feel will enhance your loan package application.

- Logical inclusions are a copy of the sales contract on a new piece of equipment and possibly the research information you used to make your equipment selection.
- If you are moving to a new location, you would include a copy of the lease, blueprints of any construction, copies of legal documents, and even a photograph of the site.
- If you are introducing a new product or service, include a product brochure and additional market research information.
- This section also gives you the chance to put a positive slant on a negative reason for needing a loan. For instance, if you have insufficient working capital (which could look like poor planning, poor receivables collection, etc.) you could chart how your need for expanded working capital developed, thus showing your understanding of the trend, whether it's positive (increased orders) or negative (lengthening collectibles).
- If either your receivables or your payables are outstanding by more than thirty days, your banker will expect to see a chart showing the aging of those accounts. This information is presented in the chart titled "Aging of Accounts Receivable or Aging of Accounts Payable."
- If it *is* true that your collectibles are lengthening, include your plan for stepping up your collection of overdue accounts.

Aging of Accounts Receivable
or
Aging of Accounts Payable

Account	30 days	60 days	90 days	120 days	150 days	180 days
AaMachines	$110.00					
Beta Blues	$55.00	$85.00	$100.00			
Charlie Line	$100.00	$100.00				
Delta Prince			$500.00	$100.00*		
Echo Point	$45.00					
Foxtrot			$100.00		$100.00*	
Golf Addict						$85.00*
Hotel Room	$60.00		$60.00			
TOTAL:	$370.00	$185.00	$760.00	$100.00	$100.00	$85.00

List alphabetically by account name, projecting the dollar amount due in the column for number-of-days since the goods were shipped.

Your banker will expect to see attached notes on how often overdue accounts have been contacted, and what payment arrangements have been attempted.

A banker would probably ask why this company routinely permits 90-day terms. Frequently when all receivables are slow it's because invoices are not being mailed on the same day that goods are shipped or services performed. A banker might want to see specific changes to speed collections, such as offering a five or ten percent discount for payment within 10 days.

New companies, in particular, should make creative use of this section. Copies of publicity you have generated can demonstrate your ability to market your product. The written comments of a Service Corps of Retired Executives (SCORE) or Small Business Development Center (SBDC) counselor on how you should fine-tune your business plan can work to your advantage by showing that you are utilizing all your resources in your endeavor to run your business successfully. While even the most glowing assurance from your largest customer, in writing, that your services are valued won't make a banker overlook weak financials, it too can underscore your potential.

They are all selling tools.

CHECKLIST: HOW CAN YOU STRENGTHEN YOUR BUSINESS PLAN/LOAN APPLICATION PACKAGE?

☐ What is the purpose of my business? Why did I start it and where do I want it to go?

☐ Is my business on track? Is it growing in the direction I envisioned when I began?

☐ Will the funds I'm requesting further my business's growth toward my goals?

☐ What assets (cash, semiliquid, property) can I use to prove my commitment and reliability?

☐ What's the best way to document or prove the management expertise and industry know-how in my business?

☐ Do we have the skills and expertise that will be needed to implement our next phase successfully?

☐ What distinct advantages does this business enjoy (location, home based, customer profile, market niche)?

☐ What obstacles are ahead that we should be thinking about now?

☐ What opportunities are ahead that can work to our advantage?

☐ Are any major risks associated with our product, service, industry, market, or people? How can we minimize these risks?

☐ Does our product or service serve a growing or declining need? What additional markets could be available to us? What adaptations must we make to service these markets?

☐ Are we in the right location to best service our customers?

9

Presenting Your Bottom Line

Why are bankers so insistent on extensive sets of financials? Why do they want to see income statements and balance sheets for three years past? Why, just when you think the loan is about to be approved, do they call and ask for additional figures for five years past? Don't they understand that you have a great product and know how to sell it, and that's enough?

UNDERSTANDING YOUR FINANCIALS

According to banker Roger Bel Air, author of *How to Borrow Money From a Banker*, "I know of many cases in which financial planning was the key ingredient in turning around a marginally profitable operation. This is because financial planning charts the course for a company. It outlines in quantifiable terms where you are now and where you want to be. Once objectives are set, you can allocate the resources necessary to reach your goals."

If those are not sufficient reasons to learn to read your financials, have you ever asked your accountant, or yourself, these questions: How did this summer compare with last year's? Am I making more or less profit than my competitors? How fast can I grow? Can I afford to hire more people? Should I do an ad campaign? Can I afford an ad campaign? Can I raise wages by four percent this year? Will my cash dry up if I accept a really large order? If we are doing so well, why do we have to scrape to pay our monthly bills? When I ask for a line-of-credit, why does my banker say I need equity capital?

These questions really are answerable. You just have to look in the crystal ball that's sitting on your desk right now—remember, the financial statements your accountant gave you last April? They really are worth more than a quick glance to confirm that you are making a profit. In fact, they will reveal the answers to many of the questions entrepreneurs ask, as well as indicate how you can cut your costs and increase your profits.

Far too many business owners find financial statements too dry to pay attention to and too difficult to analyze. In fact, too many business owners just don't look at them at all. Bankers have come to anticipate that the majority of entrepreneurs have a mindset that makes them reluctant to examine their financials. But, says one banker, "We also know from experience that every successful entrepreneur understands and uses financial reports."

Not only is the success of your business dependent on understanding your financials, learning to use them can be fascinating and revealing. What's more, we promise to make the effort painless by taking you through the steps with the help of the fictitious company known as Sourpuss's Ultimate Lemonade Stand, something it seems every entrepreneur dreamed of owning back in the days when Mom paid the expenses and the income was pure profit. As we explain the steps, get out your own financial statements and make the same calculations for your business.

THE BALANCE SHEET

If this is the first time you have analyzed your financial statements, you should look for the big picture. Start with your latest balance sheet—it's the one with two side-by-side columns showing your business's *Assets* on the left and *Liabilities* on the right. It's a formal document—which just means that it always shows the same information in the same order, whether it's reporting on a multinational company or on Sourpuss's Ultimate Lemonade Stand.

As you can see from Sourpuss's Balance Sheet, under the Liabilities column on the right there is a third section, showing the difference between the assets and liabilities as her business's *Net Worth*, or Sourpuss's equity. Net worth increases as profits accumulate in the business. Twenty percent of Sourpuss's start-up capital came from her brother, Tom Cat, so his equity share is also shown.

Items in Sourpuss's Assets column are listed from most liquid (cash) at the top, to least liquid (real estate) at the bottom. Entries are grouped under current assets, those that represent cash (bank accounts, accounts receivable, inventory and prepaid expenses) and fixed assets, those that are not converted to cash during normal operation of the business.

The Liabilities column is arranged in order of decreasing immediacy, from the most pressing debts (accounts payable) to the least pressing (the debt with the longest term). These entries are separated into current liabilities, those items that must be paid during the next twelve months, and long-term liabilities.

Return on Investment

If a single balance sheet is like a snapshot of a business, comparing a series of these statements adds the richness of watching a movie. From several sheets we can extract trends that, if they continue, predict the future of the business. We can also extract relationships and compare them to industry averages to show the current health of the business.

Now is the time to get out your balance sheets for the last three to five years and lay them out on your desk in chronological order. As we consider Sourpuss's Ultimate Lemonade Stand, you can also discover if similar trends are apparent in your business.

Let's start with a simple trend. The Ultimate Lemonade Stand's current balance sheet tells us where the business's as-

BALANCE SHEET
The Ultimate Lemonade Stand as of 12-31-95[1]

Assets[2]		Liabilities[7]	
Current assets[3]		**Current liabilities**[5]	
Cash on hand	$500	Accounts payable	$200
Inventory		Bill for sugar: $50	
Lemonade supplies	$500	Corner rent: $150	
Total:	*$1,000*	**Short-term debt**[6]	
		12 × $50 payments on	
		orange grove	$600
Fixed assets[4]			
Equipment		*Total:*	*$800*
Lemonade stand	$2,000		
Fancy Juicer	$2,000	**Long-term liabilities**	
Orchards		Mortgage on	
Mature lemon trees	$4,000	orange grove	$1,200
Maturing orange			
trees	$3,000		
		Total liabilities:	**$2,000**
Total:	*$11,000*		
		Net worth	
		Owner's equity—80%	$8,000
		Investor's equity—20%	$2,000
		Total equity:	***$10,000***
		Total liability &	
Total assets:	**$12,000**[8]	***net worth:***	**$12,000**[8]

[1] Always as at a specific date.

[2] Listed from most liquid at top to least liquid at bottom.

[3] Represents cash.

[4] Items not converted to cash in normal operation.

[5,6] Due within next twelve months.

[7] Listed in order of decreasing immediacy.

[8] Always equal.

sets are allocated. Sourpuss can see that her initial $6,000 investment has grown to $10,000. As Sourpuss is drawing a salary that's commensurate with what she would be paid managing a street stand, she calculates that her accumulated net worth is a 66 percent return on her initial investment.

But we can refine this information: Sourpuss started her lemonade stand with the expectation of selling it in five years and using the equity to manufacture pinball machines. For the last three years, she has paid expenses and bought two groves of fruit trees, yet she still has money in the bank and some fancy juicing equipment. She knows the stand is profitable, but will its sale finance a pinball enterprise?

To find out, divide the net worth on each balance sheet by the net worth for the previous year. This will give the percentages by which the equity increased, or decreased, that year or the **return on investment** (ROI) figure.

The equity in the lemonade stand at 12/31/95 was $10,000, at 12/31/94 it was $8,500, and at 12/31/93 it was $7,300. Sourpuss started the stand with $6,000. Therefore the equity increased by 21 percent the first year, 16.4 percent the second year, and 17.6 percent the third year. If Sourpuss can continue to build the owner's equity at an average of 18 percent a year (an annual ROI of 18 percent is her newest business objective), she figures it will be three more years before that equity will finance the pinball machine operation. That's a year more than she wanted to wait, but now she knows what her lemonade stand is capable of achieving.

A Broader Perspective

When Sourpuss showed the balance sheet to Tom Cat, he pointed out that the orchards were listed at historical value (the amount Sourpuss paid for them) and that they would now sell for more. He also argued that a smart lemonade stand on a busy corner would have a goodwill value equal to a year's profit.

Tom Cat's points are good ones, but he sometimes talks through his whiskers, so Sourpuss called a business broker and discovered that there is, indeed, a standard multiplier for estimating the goodwill of lemonade stands. However, its use depends on how her business compares with similar operations.

What Does It Mean?

"Spiffier and nicer customers," was Sourpuss's first thought; "How it compares would be nice to know," was her second. So she called her accountant and her banker and eventually tracked down some industry averages for street-corner beverage stands.

In Appendix C under "Bibliography" you'll find sources of financial ratios for industries ranging from advertising to video stores. Many of the industry averages are compiled in the *Annual Statement Studies* and *Industry Norms & Key Business Ratios*, which good business libraries carry.

Bankers Look at Ratios

One of the first industry averages Sourpuss encountered was the **current ratio** or **working capital ratio** figure that indicates the solvency of a business: the company's ability to pay its bills. To figure this ratio, *divide your current assets by your current liabilities.*

Sourpuss's balance sheet shows current assets of $1,000 and current liabilities of $800, so her working capital ratio is 1.25:1— she has $1.25 for each $1 she owes. Sourpuss thinks this is quite healthy, although her industry average is 1.50:1 and her banker would probably want to see a 2:1, or even a 3:1, ratio before writing a loan.

Bankers also figure an **acid-test ratio** (or quick ratio) by dividing only the cash and accounts receivable by the current liabilities. This can give a very different picture of a business's solvency. The acid-test ratio for Sourpuss's business ($500 divided by $800) is .63:1, so if Sourpuss's creditors became demanding and she couldn't sell her inventory fast enough, her apparently healthy enterprise could go out of business!

Whenever the acid-test ratio is below 1:1, a business owner needs to ask whether backup financing may be needed. The answer lies in why the acid-test ratio is out of balance. For instance, is current inventory exceptionally high? If so, why? A projected cash crunch from pre-Christmas buildup of stock has short-term consequences, which may be alleviated with a line-of-credit. However, unsold inventory from a poor summer may have to be liquidated at a loss or carried until the next summer. To make this decision, you would need to compare storage costs with the actual cost of your inventory; and this brings us to the second essential financial statement, the income statement.

THE INCOME STATEMENT
(OR THE P & L)

The income, or profit-and-loss (P & L), statement is also a formal document—it always shows the same information in the same order. But where a balance sheet shows the condition of a company on a specific date (such as the end of each month, quarter, or financial year), an income statement shows the progress of the company during a specific period. Income statements may be prepared annually or quarterly, but they can be especially valuable when prepared monthly and compared with a cash flow forecast.

Sourpuss's income statement is the simplest form of P&L. In the top section, net sales less the cost of goods sold equals the gross profit for the month shown. In the second section, the amount for general and administrative expenses is deducted from gross profit to arrive at the operating profit for the period covered; other income or expenses are added or deducted to calculate the net profit before taxes.

If this is what your P&L looks like, you'll need to expand it before it will serve as a truly effective management tool. For in-

INCOME STATEMENT
The Ultimate Lemonade Stand
for October 1995 *

Sales		
Net sales (4,000 units)	$4,000	
Cost of goods sold	$2,000	
Gross profit		*$2,000*
Expenses		
General and administrative expenses	$1,300	
Total operating expenses:		$1,300
Operating profit		*$700*
Other income		
Interest	$25	
*Net** profit before taxes*		*$725*

* May be for a month, a quarter, or a year, but always for a period of time.

** Still getting *gross* and *net* confused? Net is what's caught in the net for the IRS to fish from, after everything except taxes is calculated.

stance, last year lemonade was Sourpuss's only product, but recently she began selling fresh squeezed orange juice to morning commuters. If she codes her cash receipts as either orange juice or lemonade, she can show under net sales how much business she does in each product, thereby tracking their comparative success.

Similarly, under her cost of goods sold, she needs separate line entries for the costs of harvesting fruit, purchased ingredients, and plastic cups and napkins, since these are all supplies that vary according to the number of drinks, or units, sold. With this information, Sourpuss could calculate her direct costs for each drink.

Margins Are Magic

When she started her business, Sourpuss simply priced her lemonade by adding a reasonable profit to the direct cost of each drink. She knew that the difference between her costs and her selling price had to cover her overhead before she started making a profit, but she didn't know how many glasses of juice she had to sell before her lemonade stand would begin to make a profit.

Tom Cat pointed out that the actual cost of her product adds the variable costs (shown under cost of goods sold) to the fixed costs or overhead (shown under general and administrative expenses). He explained that the **contribution margin** is the amount contributing first to fixed costs, then to profit. Tom Cat demonstrated how this is figured by taking the $1 per unit sales price and deducting 50 cents per unit for direct costs to arrive at a contribution margin of 50 cents per unit. Next, Tom Cat divided Sourpuss's fixed costs ($1,300) by the contribution margin (50 cents) to arrive at the number of units (2,600) Sourpuss needed to sell to break even.

After Sourpuss figured her break-even point, she wondered if her profit per unit was increasing or decreasing. By calculating each year's variable costs as a percentage of net sales and each year's fixed cost as a percentage of gross profit, Sourpuss had ratios that she could compare. These ratios showed a trend of annual decreases in her variable costs, which reflected the savings she made by growing her own fruit. But it shocked Sourpuss to find that maintaining her orchard was pushing her fixed costs up at a much faster rate and causing her profit margin to shrink. Nevertheless, when Sourpuss compared these trends with her industry averages for the same three years, she found she was doing better than her competitors.

For Sourpuss to decrease her costs she must also expand her income statements to include line entries for each major item included in general and administrative expenses. In addition, she needs a cash flow forecast, based on a budget.

FORECASTING YOUR CASH FLOW

A budget is a simple list of expenses projected for a specific period or project such as a year or an advertising campaign. A cash flow forecast, or budget, spreads the projected expenses over a time sheet, thus showing when funds will be needed.

To calculate a budget for the coming year, start by comparing the annual increases for each line item. For instance, in preparing the Cash Flow Budget on page 98, Sourpuss estimated her lemonade sales for this year by figuring the percentage increase for each of the two preceding years and assuming she would do as well as their average. Estimate those cost items with a stable trend, such as rent, by assuming the trend will continue; but estimate items under cost of goods sold (direct costs), as a percentage of anticipated sales.

These estimates give an annual budget that is turned into a cash flow forecast by projecting each item into twelve monthly installments. Such items as rent and the owner's salary can be divided by twelve for monthly entries. However, the income and costs that relate to sales must be adjusted to reflect anticipated highs and lows—the seasonal and cyclical variations you've learned to expect. The easiest way to figure how much to enter for each month is to calculate the percentage of annual sales that each month's sales represented during the previous year. Then break down the estimated sales and variable costs for the coming year in a similar pattern.

Creating New Scenarios

The first great value of having a cash flow forecast is that it enables you to see how specific changes can affect the entire year.

CASH FLOW BUDGET
The Ultimate Lemonade Stand for 1996

Descriptions	Jan.	Feb.	Mar.	April	May	June	July	Aug.	Sep.	Oct.	Nov.	Dec.
Lemonade sales*	2000	2000	3000	4000	6000	8000	9000	8000	7000	5000	2000	2000
Orange sales**	3000	3000	4000	5000	6000	7000	8000	9000	8000	8000	7000	5000
Total sales	**5000**	**5000**	**7000**	**9000**	**12000**	**15000**	**17000**	**17000**	**15000**	**13000**	**9000**	**7000**
Direct costs†	2000	3000	4000	4000	8000	8000	8000	8000	7000	6000	4000	4000
Rent‡	150	150	150	150	160	160	160	160	160	160	160	160
Mortgage	600	600	600	600	600	600	600	600	600	600	600	600
Wages§	—	—	—	—	500	500	500	500	300	—	—	—
Monthly income	**2250**	**1250**	**2250**	**4250**	**2740**	**5740**	**7740**	**7740**	**6940**	**6240**	**4240**	**2240**
Cumulative monthly income:	2250	3500	5750	10000	12740	18480	26220	33960	40900	47140	51380	53620
Average-to-date monthly income:	2250	1750	1916	2500	2548	3080	3745	4245	4544	4714	4670	4468

*Lemonade sales: For 1996, Sourpuss increased her 1995 figures by the same percentage of increase from 1994 to 1995 and rounded her figures downward.

**Orange sales: With just three months of orange sales in 1995, Sourpuss used the month-to-month increases from her first year of lemonade sales to project what her monthly increases might be in 1996. She hopes that summer heat will provide the same increased volume for orange juice as for lemonade and that orange juice will sell more steadily in the cooler winter months.

†Direct costs: Sourpuss has learned to buy supplies ahead of the hot weather to avoid being caught short by an early summer.

‡Rent: Sourpuss has projected the same annual increase as for previous years.

§Wages: Wages are based on the average number of hours of assistance needed in previous summers, at what Sourpuss believes will be the prevailing hourly rate for teens this summer.

For instance, suppose each of your salespeople is working on retainer and commission, writing an average of 150 times their earnings in orders, and that the average period from receipt of order to payment of account is seventy days. If you add a new salesperson in February, you would have fixed retainer costs through to December, but commission costs would be delayed until orders were received and not start until March or April. Income from these sales would probably not start until April or May, but costs of the goods sold might increase as early as March. By doing such calculations on a computer spreadsheet, you can quickly estimate how much additional cash you would require in the first and second quarter, and how quickly (third or fourth quarter) you could pay it back. This type of understanding of your operations is exactly what your banker is looking for when he or she evaluates your request for a line-of-credit.

Although you can do this type of forecasting with paper and pencil, it's well worth investing the time and effort needed to learn a basic spreadsheet program. Once you have mastered having the computer figure how quickly costs and sales increase after the implementation of an ad campaign, the hiring of a new salesperson, or the installation of a new piece of equipment, you'll wonder how you managed your business without such forecasting. Once again, this type of understanding of your operation is exactly what your banker is looking for when he or she evaluates your request for a line-of-credit.

Effecting Those Scenarios

The second great value of a cash flow forecast is the way it will help you to manage your business on a daily basis. Have your bookkeeper supply monthly income statements showing two sets of figures—the figures for the current month and the total from the beginning of the year. Each month compare these with your cash flow forecast to see what actually happened compared with what you predicted would happened. No, "perfect" is *not* having them match on a month-to-month basis. Perfect is *adjusting the forecast*. Perfect is catching the unexpected (whether good or bad) as soon as it starts to show itself. Then you can take corrective action either by capitalizing on an upsurge in sales or by investigating an increase in costs immediately.

If there's one type of borrower that bankers love, it's the entrepreneur who comes in saying, "My figures are showing an increase in orders that could lead to a shortage of cash next quarter. Can we increase our line-of-credit to cover ourselves? It looks like we will be in a good position for payback the following quarter." The banker will be especially happy if the entrepreneur has the figures to back up that statement!

In using your cash flow forecast, remember the words of banking consultant Roger Bel Air: "A plan is only a plan, and accuracy in numbers isn't as important as knowing why there is a discrepancy." Discrepancies can occur because your company received an unexpectedly large order, or didn't receive an expected order. When you track your business with financial statements, any changes, whether caused by severe weather or fresh competition, will show up quickly enough for you to take action to reduce the damage.

Do It with an Expert

Although you are encouraged to learn to read your financials and use them consistently, you probably shouldn't go it alone. Every business needs a competent accountant, and such an accountant is the ideal person to help you evaluate your progress and set realistic, achievable goals. Spending a few hours with your accountant on a regular basis is one of the best investments you can make. Until you are proficient at reviewing your statements, an hour or two a month is not too much. As you become proficient, a quarterly meeting supplemented by brief phone calls will probably suffice. (If you really can't afford this time with your accountant, see Chapter 15, "Back to Basics," for some low-cost alternatives.) By reviewing your statements with your accountant, and learning some of the other ratios by which you can track the trends most appropriate to your business, you will ensure that you manage your business rather than have it manage you. And probably nothing will convince your banker of your creditability faster than your obvious understanding of what those figures mean. (If we could find yet another way to say this, we would!)

Using Cash Flow Projections

One way to use cash flow projections is to see how profit changes with a decrease in costs versus an increase in price.

Lemonade sales:	at $1 per unit =	$2000
Orange sales:	at $1 per unit =	$3000
Total sales:		$5000
Direct costs:	at 50¢ each =	$2500
Gross profit	= 50 percent	$2500

Lemonade sales:	at $1 per unit =	$2000
Orange sales:	at $1 per unit =	$3000
Total sales:		$5000
Direct costs:	at 45¢ each =	$2250
Gross profit	= 55 percent	$2750

Lemonade sales:	at $1.05 each=	$2100
Orange sales:	at $1.05 each=	$3150
Total sales:		$5250
Direct costs:	at 50¢ each =	$2500
Gross profit	= 52+ percent	$2750

As you can see, for the same gross profit in dollars, a decrease in costs of five cents per unit would increase gross profits to 55 percent, whereas an increase in price of the same five cents per unit results in less than 2½ percent increase in gross profits.

HOW MUCH CAN YOUR BUSINESS PAY YOU?

One of the most frustrating aspects of business ownership for neophyte entrepreneurs is not knowing how much the business can afford to pay them for their long hours of work. For the person who is used to a regular corporate salary and has high hopes for a new business, the month that "leaves nothing for me" can be disappointing as well as frustrating.

Bankers are also apt to look closely at the amount an entrepreneur has been drawing from the business. Yes, they do realize that you have no wish to work for nothing! But they also know that for a business to survive, its cash needs have to be put before the owner's needs.

Sourpuss was advised to create her cash flow budget (page 98) without a line for owner's draw (or salary) in order to see more clearly what her business could afford. Assuming her predictions are accurate, Sourpuss's Ultimate Lemonade Stand will average more than $4,000 a month in profits this year, but it will be August before Sourpuss can draw that much. However, the forecast shows that she could draw as much as $1,500 a month from the beginning of the year and either increase her draw monthly or quarterly or take a lump sum from the business at the end of the year.

But Sourpuss is "tired of scraps or salmon" in her personal life, so she took her projections to her banker and asked for a line-of-credit to be used to even out the lean and fat months. After verifying the trends on which Sourpuss based her predictions, Ms. Leonine, the banker, asked why Sourpuss hadn't left the profits from the previous year in the business to be drawn during the slow months? Sourpuss explained that she needed those profits to pay off a personal line-of-credit, which she'd taken the previous winter when the lemonade stand's receipts were low. Finally, Ms. Leonine agreed to make the loan because, she said, "I can see you are learning to run your business on a fiscally responsible basis."

CHECKLIST: WHAT DOES YOUR BUSINESS NEED NOW?

☐ How much does the company have invested in capital expenses?

☐ How much can we reliably expect from sales?

☐ How are our sales growing compared to projected sales?

☐ How much income can we expect from other sources?

☐ How do our costs of supplies compare with projected costs?

☐ How do general expenses compare with projected expenses?

☐ Where can we trim expenses without cutting income and profit potential?

☐ How much do we need now? In the next three months? Six months? One year?

☐ What long-term financing do we need? Over the next year? Three years? Five years? Ten years?

☐ When will we need funding again? What are the financial steps of our projected growth?

☐ Is our need for funding a recurring, cyclical need?

☐ How much do we need? Who offers that size amount?

☐ How long do we need it for? Who offers that time period?

10

Negotiating the Best Loan

POINTS OF INTEREST

The following story is true. The banker wishes to remain anonymous.

"Recently, a local businessman came in to talk about financing a new venture. This is a small town with a tiny airstrip, and he wanted to buy a small plane and offer scenic rides over our valley and coast. Because the town does get a lot of weekend tourism, I said I'd consider it.

"Within a few days I called and offered him a loan. I told him what the terms of the loan would be. He asked if I'd be free at noon, and I thought he wanted to do lunch to celebrate. He picked me up and drove out to the airstrip where there's a dinky little eatery. He bought me a sandwich and a cup of coffee and led the way to this tiny crate he called a plane. I gulped down the hot coffee before we were off the ground and tried to think of all the questions I knew I should ask about small-plane safety.

"But it's seductive up there, with the farms neatly lined up below and the trees turning red. Pretty soon I relaxed and congratulated myself on writing a profitable loan for the bank. I figured he'd do just about anything to be able to fly that plane every day. So when he said the interest rate was a bit steep, I just laughed. I figured he'd pay it.

"Then he looped the loop."

By the time they reached the ground, the interest rate was half a point lower.

The message: you can get a lower interest rate—though it's probably not necessary to loop the loop with your banker to do so. According to Roger Bel Air (not the banker of the story), "The most important thing to remember about interest rates is that they are negotiable." Bel Air calls this, "the bankers' secret."

"Eighty-five to 90 percent of all business borrowers accept the loan terms their bankers' offer," comments a banker. "Yet about 60 percent of all businesses could get a lower interest rate if they asked for it."

Negotiating the cost of your loan—the combination of interest rate and points—is as important as negotiating a better price with your suppliers. For example, suppose your banker offers you a $200,000 term loan at 7.5 percent and you can negotiate it down to 7 percent. That half percent will save your business $1,000 a year.

"Of course, if you are barely profitable and not well capitalized, you'll be lucky to get a loan at all," points out another banker. "The business owners who could negotiate lower rates are the ones with good profits and strong financial statements."

"Yes," agrees a third banker, "To keep the business of financially strong customers, we have to give more service and be more competitive."

The right time to ask for a lower interest rate is after the banker has offered you the loan you applied for, but before the final papers have been drawn up and signed. This timing puts you in the strongest position to negotiate.

Before you meet with your banker, consider the arguments that might best work in your favor. Then ask directly, "Can you give me a lower interest rate?" If your banker demurs, or says that's the best rate he or she can offer, you need to have your strategy planned.

SEVEN FACTORS SET INTEREST RATES

To acquire your desired interest rate, you must consider the seven factors bankers consider when deciding what loan package to offer.

Cost of Funds

The bank raises capital from which to make loans by servicing deposits and institutional borrowing. Its profit and its cost of doing business, from pens to health-care insurance, is covered from the difference between what it pays depositors and what it charges borrowers.

Perception of Risk

In deciding to make the loan, your banker evaluated its risk. Having decided that the loan is sufficiently risk-free to write, your banker will set the interest rate according to how certain and hassle-free she or he thinks your payments will be. The more creditworthy you are, the less your loan will cost.

Repayment

Believe it or not, bankers have no better idea of the future cost of money than you do. Therefore, to a banker the longer the term of the loan (number of months), the riskier the loan is. Bankers don't like to find themselves with their assets loaned out at 7 percent when they could be getting 9 or 11 percent.

Amount Being Borrowed

You've heard it before: It takes the same amount of time to review and process a large loan as it does to review and process a small loan. The cost of loan processing is directly reflected in the cost of loans, so the more you borrow, the more you benefit from having the bank's cost of writing your loan spread over a greater number of dollars. Getting a small loan today, and another small loan in six months, simply doubles your bankers' costs without doubling his or her profits.

Handling Costs

Of course, small loans don't take precisely the same amount of time to review and write, but the variables dictated by risk are much greater than those dictated by dollar amount. Therefore, if your business qualifies for an unsecured loan, your interest rate will be lower than if the bank requires collateral—not just because you are perceived as being less risky, but because the collateral you secure the loan with has to be precisely documented and possibly monitored.

For instance, if you pledge your receivables and inventory as collateral for a line-of-credit, their constantly changing status will require regular reports and your banker will have to check your figures and monitor your bank account. This takes time, and your interest rate will be calculated to compensate the bank.

Average Balance on Deposit

Suppose you deposit $56,000 each week and write checks for $50,000. Very little of your money stays in your account. If your neighbor deposits $26,000 each week, but writes checks for only $14,000, her account is worth twice as much as yours is to the bank. Banks make money on the deposits that stay with them; the rest is paperwork.

Good customers keep their reserves with their bank. They use the bank's certificates of deposit instead of another financial institution's money market account. They keep their personal checking and savings accounts at the same bank branch and get their personal auto loan there, too.

If you don't habitually do this, your banker may require you to maintain a compensating balance as a condition of the loan. This could raise your costs by tying up part of your business's operating capital.

Competition

The one independent factor working in your favor is that your banker knows that if the loan is too expensive, or if the bank doesn't provide the services you need, you will be tempted to take your business elsewhere.

The Point of It All

These seven factors dictate the interest rate your banker offers and the points asked as closing costs. According to a Midwest banker: "These factors mean that the higher the risk to the bank, the higher the interest rate." She adds, "The more you borrow, the more flexibility your banker has."

FOUR TECHNIQUES THAT CAN LOWER LOAN COSTS

From the previous discussion it should be clear that the most effective way to negotiate a lower interest rate is to make your loan less risky for the banker. The straightforward approach is to say, "What can I do to make the loan easier for you to write?"

There are four principal answers to this question.

1. **Accept a shorter loan period.** The shorter your loan period the less risk there is to the bank. So if you think you could pay off the loan in less time, you may be able to negotiate a lower interest rate for the shorter term.

2. **Improve the quality of your collateral.** Although bankers do write loans on equipment and inventory, they prefer collateral such as home equity and common stock. Bankers expect the threat of losing a home to motivate the borrower to pay off the loan even if the business goes under. Common stock is appreciated provided the bank can hold the stock certificates and sell them quickly if you default on the loan.

3. **Increase your deposits.** As a hedge against your defaulting, long-term deposits can be highly acceptable to the bank

whether pledged as collateral or not. And if pledged you are still able to keep intact monies you have set aside for a special purpose, such as your child's college account.

4. **Improve your personal standing with your banker.** If your business is a corporation, you could offer to personally guarantee the loan. If your company has financial investors, you could have one of them guarantee the loan. Certainly you should emphasize the fact that you are a loyal customer by mentioning the years you have been using the bank's services, your home mortgage with their parent company, and the timeliness of your auto loan payments.

Bankers agree, the business you have done with a branch over the years is all to your credit.

CHECKLIST: HAVE YOU CONSIDERED THE DOLLARS AND SENSE?

☐ How much does this money cost? Can I handle the repayment schedule and still make a profit?

☐ Does it make sense for me to get this loan at this cost?

☐ Does the line-of-credit have to be zeroed (fully paid off) once every year, every three years, or never?

☐ If I am late with a payment, what will the consequences be?

☐ Is a large balloon payment due at any point? Will I be able to pay it if refinancing is not available?

☐ What collateral will I have to put up?

☐ If the bank repossesses the collateral, will that finalize the debt?

☐ What will I owe if my business goes under?

11

Government Assistance Is Not Welfare

Whether you are an experienced business owner or a neophyte in the planning or startup stage, you've undoubtedly heard a great deal about Small Business Administration (SBA) loans. Yet, much of what you may "know" is probably not true. There seem to be more myths about SBA loans than about any other type of business financing. Blame it on the fact that the SBA puts its loan money to work financing businesses rather than educating the public on what it has to offer.

The first myth to explode is that there are such things as SBA grants. There are none: not for startups, not for established businesses, not for special projects, not for defense cuts, not to minorities, not to women, and not to the disadvantaged.

The second myth is that there are easy-to-get, inexpensive loans for any of the situations or people just mentioned, and that you can apply directly to the SBA for one. This is also not true.

The third myth is that to get an SBA loan (actually a loan guarantee), your application for a loan has to be turned down by one, three, five, or twenty-five banks. Not true. Then there are all the other myths.

TYPES OF SBA LOANS

Let's go to the facts. The SBA's financial efforts to help small-business owners get financing essentially falls into three categories:

1. Direct loans in declared disasters
2. A variety of loan guarantee programs for low-to-moderate financing needs under the 7(a) umbrella
3. A loan guarantee program for major financing under the 504 program

Direct Loans for Victims of a Declared Disaster

These loans are made through SBA on-site offices, at very low interest rates (with delayed initial payments when requested), to enable businesses damaged by the disaster to recover as quickly as possible. Disasters include floods, hurricanes, earthquakes, and anything else that prompts a state's governor to officially request that the President declare the affected region a disaster area. If you should find yourself in such a situation, you should contact the SBA on-site office for assistance.

Here is the most important warning about preparing for such a disaster: An SBA spokesperson warns that "The one thing which most often delays the processing of applications is lack of documentation. If a business is totally destroyed, it may be that the only attainable documentation is in the form of tax returns, which have to be requested from the IRS. Other documentation—evidence of machinery, sales, loans, etc.—may be completely destroyed and have to be pieced together *by the applicant*, in a long, grueling process of telephone calls and letters."

In Appendix D, "Protecting Your Business from Disaster," you will find specific suggestions for ensuring that your business has the documentation you need in the event of *any* disaster.

Loan Guarantee Programs Under the 7(a) Umbrella

The SBA has been guaranteeing bank loans to small businesses since it was created by Congress in 1953. In 1989 more than 18,000 loans, amounting to approximately $3 billion, were made, and the total rose to 55,590 loans in 1995, worth $7.8 billion.

In recent years, the number of lenders willing to make SBA loans has increased to more than 8,000, and they are located throughout the country. Of these, some 660 are certified lenders (who process 30 percent of all SBA loans) and 156 are preferred lenders. Certified lenders have received special training so that they can do much of the processing required by the SBA in-house, thus cutting down on the time it takes to get SBA approval from approximately two weeks to three days. Preferred lenders have received additional training plus certification, which authorizes them to give in-house approval for an SBA guarantee of up to 80 percent of the loan amount. Preferred lenders must have their authority renewed every two years, and such loans are essentially restricted to borrowers with very strong credit.

However, for most businesses, an SBA loan application will go through the business's regular banker, as a result of that bankers' saying that the bank alone cannot make the requested loan but will do so with a cosigner, such as the SBA. If your banker turns down your loan application without suggesting this type of arrangement, ask what you can do to strengthen your creditworthiness, at least to the point of qualifying for an SBA loan guarantee.

In the probably rare instance when your banker says your bank does not process SBA loans, you would be justified in calling the SBA's Answer Desk and requesting a list of local certified lenders. Note that having your banker state that her or his bank does not process SBA loans is quite different from hearing that your loan application would not even qualify for an SBA loan. The one justifies seeking a different banker, but the other mandates that your creditworthiness be strengthened or that you acknowledge that you already have as much debt as you can carry.

Guaranteed Loans

Collectively, the various programs under the 7(a) umbrella provide bankers with a "guarantee," which significantly reduces the bank's risk and makes the loan feasible.

Guarantee.   The "guarantee" is that the SBA will compensate the bank for between 70 and 90 percent of the loan if you fail to make your payments, thereby reducing the bank's risk to between 10 and 30 percent of the amount advanced. (Different programs and loan amounts dictate a variety of SBA guarantees.) However, this is taxpayer money that is being put at risk, and the SBA usually requires additional collateral to protect its interests.

Dollar Amounts.   Recent additions to the 7(a) group of programs mean that loans from as low as $250 can now be made. In practical terms, banks are making SBA-guaranteed loans from a few thousand dollars up to $1 million, with the SBA providing a 75 percent guarantee ($750,000 on $1 million). The SBA will also guarantee up to $750,000 on loans of more than $1 million.

Terms.   These loans may be used for any of the following:

- Working capital with five- to seven-year terms
- Machinery and equipment with ten-year terms (provided that ten years does not exceed the expected life of the equipment)
- Real estate, major renovation, or the purchase of an existing business with terms of up to twenty-five years.

Terms of this length give the borrower from two to five years longer than straight bank financing to pay off a loan, which significantly reduces the risk of a too onerous payment schedule. Payments generally include monthly installments of principal and interest, with no balloon payments and no prepayment penalties. If there is an income-related reason for delaying the first payment for up to six months, the SBA will consider such a request. Working capital loans may be lines-of-credit, and if so written they must revolve; they cannot be drawn down in the beginning and paid off at the end of the term.

Interest Rates. Under most of its programs, the SBA currently restricts banks from requesting more than the following interest rates:

* *On loans of less than $25,000:*
4.25 points over the prime rate for loans of up to seven years
4.75 points over prime for loans of seven years or more
* *On loans of between $25,000 and $50,000:*
3.25 points over the prime rate for loans of up to seven years
3.75 points over prime for loans of seven years or more
* *On loans of more than $50,000:*
2.25 points over the prime rate for loans of up to seven years
2.75 points over prime for loans of seven years or more

The higher rates on loans of less than $25,000, and on loans of between $25,000 and $50,000, are allowed specifically to encourage bankers to make those smaller loans, which they usually maintain are uneconomical.

Collateral. The SBA prefers the borrower to pledge sufficient collateral to cover its portion of the loan, and it is unlikely that the bank would write the loan with anything less than 100 percent worth of pledged assets.

Other Details. Factors such as whether interest rates are fixed or variable may be negotiated by the lender and the borrower. Some programs require greater loan monitoring than others, including field visits to inspect collateral.

Eligibility. Startups are some of the hardest businesses to finance conventionally, but the SBA believes they are worth the extra effort and increased risk. You may have to pay the maximum interest the SBA allows for a startup loan (especially if the amount you are requesting is less than $50,000), but your application will be seriously considered instead of being instantly rejected. Nevertheless, strong personal creditworthiness will still be a great advantage.

Although some SBA programs are targeted to ensure that minorities, women, veterans, and disadvantaged people have access to loan guarantees, your eligibility is determined by what you do, not who you are. Eligible businesses include retailers, service firms, distributors, wholesalers, manufacturers, and exporters. Only real estate developers and gambling enterprises are ineligible for SBA-guaranteed financing.

Since SBA programs are targeted to small businesses, there are maximum size limits to ensure that programs are not exhausted by the demands of large corporations. In addition, only the Disaster Relief program is available to nonprofit organizations, and none of the SBA's programs are available to people on parole or probation.

SBA Restrictions. As with any bank loans, SBA-guaranteed loans must be used for the purpose for which they are granted. And you cannot get an SBA-guaranteed loan just to get a lower interest rate nor specifically to pay off current creditors who are complaining that they have insufficient security. Nor may an SBA-guaranteed loan be used to pay off loans or investments from relatives or friends.

Obviously, your character and your business's financials must still be good enough to convince your banker that you can, and will, repay the loan. These programs are intended to decrease the risk to bankers so that they will make more loans to small businesses, but preferably without putting taxpayers at risk of having to pay off bad debts. In fact, with a loss rate of just 1.3 percent the SBA is on a par with banks at preventing loss of their investment capital.

Preparing Your Loan Application. The SBA actually has at least one program with a single-page application that requires a minimum of attachments in the way of financial documentation!

But, this application is essentially reserved for entrepreneurs with strong credit or for the purchase of an existing business.

For most of its loan guarantees, the SBA provides the following list of items to include in your application:

- Statement explaining how the loan will be used
- History of the business
- Three years of financial statements (balance sheets and income statements)
- A schedule of term debts
- A schedule showing the aging of accounts receivable
- A schedule showing the aging of payables
- Details of your lease or property ownership
- A statement of owner's equity
- Income projections
- Expense projections
- Cash flow projections demonstrating that profits will pay off the loan
- Personal financial statements
- Personal resumes

In actuality, preparing your application for SBA review seldom requires any more financial information than your banker will ask for, but could significantly benefit from additional information demonstrating your experience in your industry and in a management capacity. Bankers who are trained to process SBA loans can guide you in preparing the additional documentation, but if your banker doesn't provide such guidance you can get it from your nearest Small Business Development Center (SBDC) or Service Corps of Retired Executives (SCORE) office. SBDC and SCORE counselors are trained at putting together 7(a) loan applications, and they will review your application for free. (See Chapter 15, "Back to Basics.")

Evaluation.   One of the most important benefits of bringing in the SBA is that the emphasis it uses to evaluate your creditability differs from a bank's. The SBA officer assigned to evaluate your application will put more emphasis on the management experience you report and your background within a similar type of business. Although this calls for additional documentation, this shift in emphasis provides a crucial advantage for many small-business owners.

The SBA does like to see significant owner's equity, particularly with startups, and prefers that owner's equity be between 30 and 50 percent of the total financing. If your projected equity will be lower than this, you should discuss it with your banker.

While the SBA's evaluation of your application officially takes from three days to two weeks, this is after all of the documentation is received. In actuality, unless your application includes every piece of paper that the SBA could possibly request, you should anticipate the SBA's review taking a month.

CREATIVE SOLUTIONS FROM THE SBA

The SBA has a history of willingness to be innovative. At any time since its inception, the agency has been testing a handful of programs by operating them on a pilot basis to examine their effectiveness in meeting the needs of a particular segment of the small-business community.

One such program is the **Defense Loan and Technical Assistance Program (DELTA),** which in October 1995 was authorized for twelve months to assist companies who had been adversely affected by 1995's severe cuts in defense spending.

Test programs such as DELTA either terminate when their authorization expires, are reauthorized for an additional specified period or, when proven justified, are modified and incorporated into existing programs. It's by such methods that the SBA seeks to expand its services to small businesses whose needs are not being met by its principal programs.

The SBA started the innovative **Microloan Program** in June 1992 to provide loans from as low as $250 to those businesses that are most often dismissed and ignored by conventional lenders. Microloans are available to startups, home-based businesses, and sole proprietorships who need financing from just a few hundred dollars up to $25,000.

Unlike most other SBA programs, the Microloan Program is not administered by bankers but by nonprofit organizations. The SBA grants these nonprofit organizations ten-year loans of up to $750,000, from which to create revolving loan funds. From these funds, they must make loans to microbusinesses. The nonprofit organizations administering the loans are also eligible for a matching grant program with which to finance marketing, management, and technical assistance for their borrowers. Most of the loans made through the Microloan program are for less than $10,000, and loans of just a few hundred dollars are not unusual.

The program was initiated in June 1992 for five years. By 1995 it had grown to include 104 sites and was available in every state. It continues to grow. In order to become part of the program, organizations must demonstrate that for a period of at least one year they have successfully made small loans to entrepreneurs. The organizations selected have the ability to reach into the nooks and crannies of the communities they serve; they include Latin-, Asian-, and African-American organizations as well as development corporations targeting rural areas, women, and inner cities.

If your business fits the profile of a Microloan borrower, you should call the SBA Answer Line for a referral to the nearest organization in the program.

One Stop Capital Shops are another SBA innovation, and the first of 15 planned shops opened in Boston, Massachusetts, on November 6, 1995. One Stop Capital Shops work in tandem with state and local economic development authorities and their SBA district offices. They offer on-site access to SBA and state resources. These shops are planned as partnerships between federal (SBA), state, and private resources such as nonprofit organizations and local banks. For instance, at the Boston site the Jewish Vocational Service is administering the SBA Microloan Program.

Call the SBA Answer Line to find out if the program has a site in your area.

OTHER SPECIAL SBA PROGRAMS

The real message of the following programs is that when a segment of the small-business population has a legitimate need, the SBA tries to meet it.

- The 8-A Participant Loan Program provides funding to small companies registered in the 8-A program. The 8-A program assists economically and socially disadvantaged businesses in applying for government procurement contracts.

- The Export Working Capital Program guarantees funds for preshipment and/or postshipment working capital to enable exporting.

- The International Trade Loan Program is for businesses that can make a convincing argument that additional financing will enable them to either enter the export market or to increase their exports. It also benefits businesses that can convincingly argue that directly competitive imports have negatively affected them.

- The Energy and Conservation Loan Program provides financing for small companies engaged in energy production or conservation activities using wind, solar, hydro, grain, and biological or industrial wastes.

- Pollution Control Loans are available for the planning, designing, or installation of noise, air, or water pollution control facilities in small businesses used to collect, store, and dispose of solid and liquid waste.

- Qualified Employee Trust Loans may be used to guarantee up to $750,000 to enable (1) companies with employee stock ownership plans to use those funds for growth and development projects and (2) to enable the employees of such companies to buy out the current ownership.

- The Fishing Industry Loan Restructuring Initiative enables fishermen and seafood processing companies to restructure their existing debt.

- The Surety Bond Guarantee Program guarantees bonds for contracts of up to $1.25 million, to cover bid, performance, and payment bonds for small and emerging contractors whose applications for surety bonding have been turned down by regular commercial channels.

THE BIG BUCKS PROGRAM

Small businesses needing production facilities or heavy, expensive equipment should look to the SBA's 504 Program for assistance. In writing 504 loans, the SBA joins your bank in a three-part financial package. You, the borrower, must put up at least 10 percent of the new capital. The bank then makes a first mortgage loan of 50 percent or more of the needed capital. The SBA's portion is never more than 40 percent of the project cost and is always less than the first mortgage.

Although there is no limit to the project size, the minimum amount the SBA will lend is $50,000 and the maximum is $1 million ($1 million is 40 percent of a $2.5 million loan package). The SBA will give terms of ten years on equipment and twenty years on real estate or major reconstruction. The bank terms must be for at least seven years for equipment loans and ten years for real estate. Other terms may be negotiated between the bank and the borrower. Typically the projects financed by the 504 Program range in size from $500,000 to $2 million; the average is about $1 million. In special cases, the SBA portion of a project may be as low as $25,000.

A typical 504 financing package looks like this:

Project Details	Owner's Equity	Bank Loan	504 Financing
Percent of project	10%	50%	40%
Security		1st lien	2nd lien
Dollar amount		No limit	$50,000–$1 million
Interest rate		Variable or fixed	Fixed
Equipment terms		7 years	10 years
Real estate terms		10+ years	20 years

Eligible Businesses

These loans are targeted to small businesses that want to purchase machinery and equipment or build or buy their own facilities. These businesses may be corporations, partnerships, or proprietorships provided their net worth does not exceed $6 million and their average net profit after taxes for the previous two years did not exceed $2 million. Most businesses are eligible; the exceptions are real estate developers, financial institutions, and nonprofit companies. The SBA prefers not to finance a single-use property, such as a concrete-batch building where cement is mixed, because such a property would have limited resale potential and would be exorbitantly expensive to adapt for any other use.

Applicants for 504 loans should have been in business for at least two years, and three years is preferable. This is not the best financing source for startups, although the SBA will consider them if the owners and directors have substantial individual track records in their industry. A loan officer with a development company certified by the SBA to make 504 loans says, "With a startup, we must be convinced that the owners or directors know the business they are starting inside and out, that they know what their competitors are doing, and that they know exactly what they need, right down to pencils and paper clips."

Applications

Your application for a 504 loan includes all the items previously listed and detailed in Chapter 8, "The Perfect Loan Application," and Chapter 9 "Presenting Your Bottom Line." In addition, you should show the source of your 10 percent (minimum) financing of the new project, document your experience with your type of business, and show that you can meet the job creation requirements described under "Job Creation and CDC Objectives."

When preparing your application package for a 504 loan, you must pay particular attention to your projections. Most 504 lenders want to know that your projections are based on at least two sources, such as direct market research and industry financial data. For the latter, contact your trade association and check the business section of your local library for *Industry Norms & Key Business Ratios, Annual Statement Studies,* or the *Almanac of Business & Industrial Financial Ratios.*

Certified Development Companies

At the local level the 504 program is administered through Certified Development Companies (CDCs), which are nonprofit organizations sponsored by private interests or by state or local governments. Some of the country's four hundred CDCs operate statewide, some are local, and all have been formed to promote and assist the growth and development of business concerns in their geographical areas. CDCs are certified by the Office of Rural Affairs and Economic Development at SBA to process applications to fund projects. The funding comes from government-guaranteed debentures, which are issued on behalf of CDCs. The debentures are pooled monthly and sold through a certificate mechanism to the public market. In fiscal year 1995, 287 CDCs approved 4,509 loans totalling $1.6 billion, an increase of 16 percent over fiscal year 1994.

Timing

If you apply for an SBA 504 loan package, you need to be aware that processing the SBA portion of the loan can take weeks. Apart from the bank financing, it must be presented to your local CDC, and not until it has passed that organization's board of directors will your application go to an SBA district office. The loan may then be approved within two weeks, unless the district office requires additional documentation.

Also, if the project involves construction, you will need an interim loan because the SBA portion cannot be finalized until there is completion and occupancy. Bankers who understand the 504 process are usually willing to arrange the interim financing. If your own banker is unfamiliar with the program, or unwilling to participate, the SBA can refer you to a CDC.

Job Creation and CDC Objectives

Each project request is reviewed by the CDC's board of directors for feasibility and compatibility with their program objectives. These objectives always include the number of jobs being created, and they may also include such goals as upgrading targeted industries, renovating blighted areas, expanding export assistance to rural areas, or creating minority-owned businesses.

As for the job creation requirement, the SBA requires that each CDC's portfolio show an average of one job created or retained for each $35,000 loaned. That's the CDC's portfolio, not your project, which is an important distinction.

Your application will have the best chance of approval if you can show that you expect to hire at least one person for every $35,000 of CDC funding (exclusive of bank funding) during the first two to three years of the project. However, if your project meets one of your CDC's other objectives, that organization will probably be willing to decrease the number of jobs it requires.

CDCs can make such trades because some of the projects they finance create more than the minimum number of jobs required, and provided the CDC is meeting the SBA's requirements, it can be flexible about individual project requirements. Nationally, the SBA estimates that since 1987 the projects that have been approved and funded have created more than 476,000 jobs, or one job for each $9,100 of 504 funding.

Loan Cost

When the loan is approved, you still won't know the actual interest rate, although the CDC portion will be fixed for the full term. Interest rates for the 504 program are currently about 1 percent above Treasury rates at the time the bond is sold. The SBA sets limits on the size of the processing fees that are added to the loan and the monthly service fee that is added to the payments.

Benefits

The 504 loan program is mainly used by businesses that are ready to purchase and renovate, or build, their own facilities.

However, startups with business plans that call for an investment in heavy equipment—such as a printing plant, a canning factory, a tool and die shop, or a plastic parts molding facility—will certainly find the program worth investigating.

It could also be suitable for startups and mature businesses that need to make a significant investment in expensive, high-tech equipment, provided that equipment has a life expectancy that makes long-term financing feasible. In fact, the SBA would require a letter from the manufacturer stating that the equipment's useful life is at least ten years before accepting it as collateral for a 504 loan.

ALL SBA LOAN PROGRAMS

In providing the SBA with funding to increase the dollar amount of financing available to small businesses, Congress knows exactly what it is doing. Fifty percent of all U.S. sales involve small businesses. Fifty percent of all private sector output comes from small businesses. Large corporations may dominate the news, but they amount to a small proportion of the country's businesses. More than half the jobs in the country are with small businesses.

But most important is the fact that through boom and bust, small businesses have created jobs at a faster rate than large businesses have eliminated them. This holds true in times of a strong economy and, perhaps more important, in times of recession. Even when SBA programs don't require job creation, they are predicated on the expectation that ensuring the success of your business is ensuring the economic growth of America.

CHECKLIST: HOW WOULD YOU ANSWER TYPICAL SBA QUESTIONS IF YOU WERE SEEKING A LOAN GUARANTEE TO PURCHASE AN EXISTING BUSINESS?

☐ Why does the owner want to sell this business?

☐ Does this business have a good location?

☐ Have you talked with business owners in the area and asked what they think of this business?

☐ Is the building in good condition? Will the owner of the building transfer the lease to you at the current rental rate?

☐ Are the staff members well trained and courteous? Do they give good service?

☐ Is the stock up-to-date and in good condition?

☐ Have you talked with the company's suppliers? Would they continue to supply a new owner at the same terms?

☐ What do you particularly like about this business? What don't you like about this business?

☐ What would you want to change after purchasing this business? What is the estimated cost of the changes you would make?

☐ How does the cost of starting a new business of this type compare with buying this business?

☐ What do you think is a fair price for this business? How does this compare with what the seller is asking?

☐ Have you discussed this purchase with your attorney and with your accountant?

12

The State of State Government Assistance

"It has been estimated that by the year 2010, all existing knowledge will double approximately every ninety days," says Laurence J. Pino, president and founder of The Open University. "Some also estimate that by the year 2020, 40 percent of the entire U.S. economy will be self-employed."

"Corporate downsizing and early retirement are no longer the negatives people once thought they were. Instead, they can be opportunities for growth and financial independence if they are coupled with entrepreneurial education," says Deborah J. Bracknell, director of the National Association of Entrepreneurs.

"For example, in the last decade, the number of service-oriented businesses grew almost 40 percent, more than three times the rate of the population. Consumers could hire someone else to perform personal and business services because of higher incomes and increased purchasing power. Individual entrepreneurs and the small businesses they create provide the major source of new ideas and inventions. The time is ripe for entrepreneurs to leave the corporate ranks and act upon their ideas and visions."

You may be surprised to learn that your state legislature, and your state Department of Commerce, have been watching this trend for longer than the media have been touting it. State governments long ago recognized that the proliferation of conglomerates would leave fewer and fewer large businesses to be divided among them. In addition, the trend of businesses gobbling up other businesses was coupled with the trend of moving corporate headquarters to large cities, both here and abroad, and of moving that even more important commodity—the facility where production provides employment—into smaller, more automated facilities or even out of the country. The equation is quite simple. Without an employment base states lose population, and without population states lose their tax base.

CREATING JOBS

Every state in the country has at least one program for creating jobs, and most of the hundreds of programs are based on the fact that small businesses create more jobs, and create them faster, than any other segment of the business community. So when insufficient capital threatens to stop your business in its tracks, when your family, your friends, and your banker stop returning your calls, you should try your friendly state capital.

Every state has some type of program to assist small-business owners, and many of these programs also help startup companies. Some state programs are targeted at minorities or women, others focus on developing new industries, and all are sensitive to the necessity of assisting companies that have the potential to create jobs, especially new jobs in areas of high unemployment. Whether or not a program specifically requires the borrower to create a certain number of new jobs, the purpose is almost always to help in-state businesses increase the state's employment base.

State programs don't always provide dollars to businesses. There are programs giving direct loans and providing loan guarantees, and some of these start as low as $1,000 while others stretch into the million-dollar range. But some states are actually forbidden by their constitutions to lend state monies and have to be innovative in finding ways to finance small businesses. One such ploy is to deposit the state's own funds with banks that agree to stretch their criteria for making small-business loans.

Probably the only thing these programs have in common is that they are available only to state residents. At least, the business receiving the funds has to be situated in the state that is dispensing them.

STARTUPS FLY WITH STATE FUNDS

Oscar and Pam Riochard met and married while working in Chicago's advertising milieu. Three years ago they moved to their home state and started Quality Advertising with the help of a state program that provided 80 percent bank loan guarantees for up to ten years for working capital, property improvements, and machinery and equipment. The Riochards converted a loft, bought the sophisticated computer equipment they needed, and had the working capital to launch their enterprise. Says Oscar Riochard, "We could have started with just our own capital, but it would have been a home-based business that might have taken years to be taken seriously by top clients. With the help of the state program we were able to open in the city and have more than met our three-year projections."

When Effran Unitas started Unitas Enterprises, his dream was to provide employment for youths in the inner-city barrio where he grew up. Unitas targeted his business to provide supplies for a local army base, and he utilized a state program that lends up to $250,000 for working capital or equipment needed for filling procurement contracts. Unitas admits to working sixty-hour weeks for the first few years, but is proud of the fact that his company has employed so many Mexican-Americans. "These are mostly labor jobs," says Unitas, "but we insist that the kids are clean and tidy, we're sticklers for punctuality, and although we are bilingual, we encourage English on the floor and organize schedules so that our workers can attend English as a second language classes. We have a high staff turnover, because these young men and women go on to other jobs. But we're training them to hold down jobs, and that's what we want to see happen."

Donna Scott financed a doughnut franchise with the help of her state's program. "They make equity loans for franchise purchases where there are going to be employees," she explains. "They only give you five years to pay off the loan, which isn't nearly long enough. But by the end of the five years you have a track record that gets you long-term bank financing. And they make sure you get that long-term financing. The state's counselor was in here whenever I wanted him, advising me on staffing problems, helping me get my books straight, and doing everything he could to make sure my business succeeded."

Ginnie Mann used a state-sponsored seed fund to finance her first mail-order catalog; Paul Naylor relocated his business with long-term state funding; Sandy Knott patented her toy invention and found a manufacturer through a state program; Chet Fox installed pollution trapping equipment with a state-guaranteed bank loan; Dawn and Roger Danvers started their trophy company at a state-sponsored incubator; Victoria Tunia used a state program to show her one-of-a-kind Apple Dolls at a national gift fair and got her first substantial orders; Robert Chrysler used a state program of preferred-interest loans for manufacturing goods that had previously been imported into his state to launch his hot-water-system manufacturing plant; and Kate and Marty Carlos used a state program for employee training when they upgraded their production equipment.

THE PROOF IS IN THE GROWTH

What do California and Ohio have in common? How about Arkansas, South Carolina, and Hawaii? Answer: In the first half of 1995 these states grew new employers faster than any other states.

In the first half of 1995, the number of businesses with employees grew more than 5 percent faster than in the same period a year earlier. In 1994, new businesses with employees grew 4 percent faster than in 1993. The trend is up and rising.

California is clearly continuing to recover from its worst recession of recent years. Small employers increased by 30.5 percent in the first half of 1995, challenged by Hawaii's increase of 26.3 percent and South Carolina's increase of 22.6 percent. The SBA's fifth region, encompassing Illinois, Indiana, Michigan, Minnesota, Ohio, and Wisconsin, made a strong showing with an increase of nearly 10 percent.

"Self-employment is just the first step," says a state program administrator. "Success becomes measurable when the self-employed become employers. Then their businesses are clearly growing; they aren't just freelance earnings until retirement or new jobs kick in; it's commitment to growing a business that meets a need." State program administrators watch the figures of new employers and cheer when the one- and two-person startups they have assisted become employing companies on the way to a secure place in the economy.

HOW TO FIND YOUR STATE'S ASSISTANCE PROGRAMS

Even though getting financing through one of your state government's programs may require more steps, and even more red tape, than getting a straight bank loan, its certainly easier than obtaining startup money from a bank. A state loan official says, "I guess bankers believe that new business owners don't know what they are doing, but we think they are highly motivated to succeed. We do provide advice, refer owners to counselors, classes, or seminars to help them meet the requirements for these loans, and to make sure they succeed. Bankers can't do that; it's just not their job. But we have an obligation to our taxpayers to make sure we don't finance failures!"

To find out what state programs are available to you, contact your local Small Business Development Center (SBDC). Most SBDCs receive both federal and state funding, and have information on federal, state, and local (few, but they do exist) financing programs.

Information on state programs is also available through your local Service Corps of Retired Executives (SCORE) office. SCORE is a federally sponsored volunteer program, and SCORE offices have information on federal, state, and local financing programs. You'll find information on SBDCs, SCORE, and similar programs in Chapter 15, "Back to Basics."

You can also contact your state's Department of Commerce or Department of Economic Development through your central state government switchboard or the telephone company. Many states have regional Departments of Economic Development, which are listed in the state government pages of your local phone book.

CHECKLIST: GETTING A TAX BREAK

Circle "T" for True or "F" for False.

1. All these expenses are deductible: home, car, computer, meals, travel, education, entertainment? T F

2. You can write off 90% of new equipment up to $20,000 in the year of purchase, instead of as long-term depreciation. T F

3. Independent contractors are always preferable to employees. T F

4. The IRS cannot shut down a business; their threats are a bluff. T F

5. The IRS always wants its full bite; it's that or jail. T F

6. Not even bankruptcy cancels tax debts. T F

7. Tax deductions for home offices are no longer available. T F

8. Having a side business provides a tax shelter for other income. T F

9. Retirement plans are a great way to save taxes for the business. T F

10. The IRS disallows family paycheck deductions. T F

Answers

1. True, if you know how to claim them.
2. False. You can write off 100% up to $17,500 in 1996 and $18,000 in 1997.
3. Not if the IRS definition is different from yours!
4. False, but you can usually negotiate monthly installments and stay open.
5. False. The IRS will sometimes settle for pennies on the dollar.
6. False. You can wipe out most tax debts, but the rules are tricky.
7. False, but it is getting harder to qualify for them.
8. Not always. Losses may be challenged unless you can prove a profit motive.
9. True, in two ways: (1) contributions are tax deductible and (2) earnings are tax-deferred until withdrawn.
10. False. You can hire family if they do actual work and aren't overpaid.

Staying up-to-date on tax deductions, procedures and consequences is just good business. For more information see Appendix C for Daily's *Tax Savvy for Small Business,* and don't forget to consult your accountant before you take any major action.

13

Adventures in Financing

Even though you may prefer the known elements of bank financing, as a small-business owner you should be aware of why entrepreneurs often opt to start their businesses with venture capital.

Perhaps the most obvious reason is that the types of ventures that appeal to bankers do not appeal to investment companies, and vice versa. It's a matter of both money and risk. Bankers, by comparison with most venture capital corporations, loan small amounts and want to do so without risk. Venture capitalists, however, expect to lend or invest substantial amounts of money and are willing to undertake considerable risk to get the returns they want.

Perhaps the most important reason for using venture capital is the great cost of taking some projects from business plans to profitable enterprises—costs that simply can't be met on a budget the size of a bank loan. If, for instance, you have a unique product or service with a substantial potential market, you may need to position your company nationwide as quickly as possible, or risk having a large corporation imitate your ideas and flood the market with a similar item. Launching such a business usually requires large infusions of cash in the million-dollar range—amounts bankers and angel lenders are unwilling to commit to any single venture.

IS VENTURE CAPITAL RIGHT FOR YOU?

- If it will take more than $500,000 to launch your company, and if you will need continued investments over a period of product development or production expansion time, your venture may be of interest to a venture capitalist. On the other hand, if financing is available through a bank or from a family investor, the amounts you need are probably too small to interest an investment company.

- Running a business and raising capital are each full-time jobs. Businesses can suffer as much when an entrepreneur's time is consumed by raising capital as they do when expenses outrun income as potential is built. If you foresee the need for major refinancing within a few short years of starting your business, you should probably delay startup until all the funds are in place. This type of funding is not available from banks.

- If your project is unusual, it could be extremely interesting to a venture capitalist. A new product or service in your industry with a high possibility of accelerating profit is high on investment company wish lists. Venture capitalists are not scared away by the possibility that the product or service may be too new, or too different, for the market to accept. Unlike bankers, they don't shy away from such risky financing but instead see its great potential.

- When your company needs to grow quickly, you are most likely to get the necessary funding from an investment firm. Because bankers lend against steady and proven returns on current investment, high-growth plans are much too speculative for them. But such situations are tailor-made for venture capitalists, who prefer to make a series of investments in a company and who evaluate the success of each investment by considering product development or market penetration rather than accumulated cash.

- Venture financiers are also attracted to companies that need major investments in facilities and equipment, plus initial working capital, in order to be launched. Of course, when such companies serve proven markets and the facilities and equipment can be used as collateral, banks could be willing lenders, especially with the Small Business Administration's (SBA's) approval. However, the size of such ventures, with their need for substantial working capital in the early stages, makes them ideal for joint funding by both bank and investment company.

TWO TYPES OF VENTURE CAPITAL COMPANIES

Venture capitalists can generally be divided into two types.

Large-Project Investment Companies

The typical venture capital or investment company makes multimillion-dollar investments in large projects. Many of them are seeking investments for large pension funds, and for these companies the size of the investments they handled in the 1980s is just too small to be cost-effective in the late 1990s. These days their investments *start at* from $3 to $5 million.

Small-Business Investment Companies

Fortunately for small-business owners, there's an alternative. Small-business investment companies, or SBICs, were started by the SBA to provide leveraged equity capital for small companies. There are approximately 190 SBICs nationwide, filling the investment niche between $250,000 and $3 million, with some of the smaller SBICs willing to consider investments as low as $100,000, and a few of the larger companies looking at proposals worth $10 million.

Another 90 SBICs, known as specialized small-business investment companies, or SSBICs, invest only in businesses owned by socially and economically disadvantaged entrepreneurs, such as minorities, women, and the disabled.

In 1992 the laws covering SBICs were significantly strengthened and improved, resulting in $550 million of new private capital coming into the system in 1994-1995, more than in the previous ten years. In addition, the 76 applicants undergoing licensing in 1996 were expected to begin operations with $1 billion in new private capital. The SBIC system has been revitalized.

"Today the quality of SBICs is higher, they are larger and more sophisticated, and the companies they invest in are more likely to succeed," says a director of a New York-based SBIC. "Because it's tougher to become licensed as an SBIC today, most SBICs have better managers than in the past. That alone means they are better able to judge the quality of the investments they are making."

SBICs are independently owned, operated, and capitalized investment firms. They are licensed and regulated by the SBA, and receive some funding from the SBA, which they are expected to leverage. By the turn of the century, it's anticipated that returns from the SBA's investments will make the process of licensing and leveraging SBICs self-perpetuating. SBICs provide financing from equity to debt, including combinations of equity and debt. SBA regulations require a minimum of five years of involvement in a venture and allow each SBIC to choose from a variety of loan and equity arrangements. Most SBICs prefer subordinated debt with options to acquire stock.

SBIC money generally costs less than other venture capital financing, but the price is still variable and related to the risks inherent in the venture. SBICs may charge up to seven points over the most recent public offerings of debentures on loans; and on a combination of debt with equity investment the limit is six points. With an equity investment, the stock must be redeemed after a certain period at market or book value. The price must be related to the value of the company and cannot be an arbitrarily set multiple of the issue price or investment. Private investment companies set their own terms.

SBICs are also prohibited from taking a controlling position in small businesses—the small-business owners give up neither control nor ownership.

HOW VENTURE CAPITALISTS OPERATE

Although venture capitalists often favor existing companies that are ready to surge into a high-growth mode, many investment firms earmark a portion of their funds as seed capital. "We will invest $100,000 to help create a business plan," says the managing director of a Chicago-based investment firm. "But that would be the first step. We would expect to invest more significant amounts within three to six months. We assess the results of each investment stage before funding the next step. In fact, we set milestones in order to monitor a company's progress."

Many investment firms also favor partnerships with other investment companies. "Frequently there is more than one venture capital investor in order to share the risk," says a San Diego investment company manager. "We also benefit from the other investment company's experience and expertise; and we share the workload of monitoring the company's development."

When several investment companies finance the same business, they also serve to verify each other's due diligence—the process of confirming each item in the entrepreneur's proposal, reworking the various sales projections, and estimating the risks involved. Due diligence shows the venture capitalist whether or not to invest in a business and helps to establish the terms under which the investment will be offered.

Most private venture companies are looking for equity transactions, but a number of them will do a combination of debt and equity. This sort of packaging allows a venture capitalist to balance potential for profit with risk.

REWARDS FOR VENTURE CAPITALISTS

Competition is the main factor limiting how much return investment companies look for—competition, and an entrepreneur's good sense. Venture capitalists know that committed entrepreneurs are motivated to make their own fortunes, not to give away the store.

Investment companies seek a minimum term that is long enough for the company to show its potential, and a maximum term that will reap their hoped-for rewards. There is a saying in the venture capital business: Lemons prove themselves in less than three years, but plums (winners) usually take seven or eight years to bear fruit.

Investment firms look for a range of returns starting as low as 20 percent. They look for a potential for a 75 percent return from new products being launched by startups, because these are the riskiest ventures they finance. Their expectations are lowest when the venture is more secure and more predictable, such as when they finance a franchise. Whatever the venture, it's important that the entrepreneur carefully figure the cost of using venture capital funding.

WHAT YOU NEED FROM A VENTURE CAPITALIST

Using venture capital to finance your company is quite similar to taking on a partner. While an investment firm does not participate in the daily management of your business, it usually has a representative on your board of directors and keeps a keen eye on your progress. So it's in your best interest to look at venture financing as a partnership arrangement and to choose your investment partner carefully.

Your first priority should be to negotiate an agreement that leaves company control with your management team and that limits the circumstances under which control can pass to the investment firm. To meet this objective, you must carefully consider the consequences of both the growth clause and the failure-to-grow clause in your contract. Determine what could happen in both the worst possible scenario and the best possible scenario, as well as the most likely scenario. Each of these consequences should be something you can live with.

Nevertheless, by involving the investment firm in certain management decisions, your company can reap considerable benefits from their knowledge and contacts in specific areas of development. Most venture capital investment firms will describe the ways in which they can be of assistance early in the negotiations. They will be assessing both how much "consulting" time your management team may need from them and how receptive you are to such input. Such companies get their experience by working with many growing businesses through all the common growth crises, so you should not be shy in drawing on their expertise and connections.

In seeking financing from a venture capitalist, you want to negotiate the lowest cost of funds that is consistent with having adequate, and ongoing, financing. The minimum term of the investment company's commitment should be long enough to avoid crippling the company by an early pullout. On the other hand, you will want to be able to buy out the investment company's equity at some point. The price to be paid to redeem the investor's stock should be negotiated in the beginning as an amount relating to the value of the company, not an arbitrarily set multiple of the issue price or the original investment.

The best agreement has a buyout arrangement that gives you flexibility in how you raise the redemption money, with timing based on the company's growth. Today, you may intend to build the company to a certain size, or for a particular length of time, and then sell it to realize your profit. But five years from now you may prefer to do something quite different. You may want to take over a supplier and grow in new directions, launch a product line that you hadn't conceived of in the beginning, or simply stay with a steadily growing company.

WOOING YOUR BACKER

The proposal you present to an investment company is in many ways similar to the loan application package you would present to a banker (see Chapter 8, "The Perfect Loan Application," and Chapter 9, "Presenting Your Bottom Line"). But there are some important differences you need to keep in mind:

- Because you will undoubtedly be asking for considerably more money than you would be asking for on a bank loan application, it should come as no surprise that an investment company will require even more information and that the application package will be larger.
- This package must be based on a solid business plan of fifteen to twenty-five pages that succinctly describes your product

and its cost of production, your market and your specific marketing plan, and a complete review of the available and needed financing.

- Your proposal must demonstrate that you have a *balanced* management team. You need a team made up of people with complementary skills who can work together to keep your vision on course. Venture capitalists look for expertise in the fields of financing, production, marketing, daily management, and long-term strategizing. They also look for (and assess) a realistic evaluation of your personal strengths, as well as the strengths of your advisers and staff.

- You need an impressive management team that will withstand scrutiny, because a conscientious investment firm will check the background of every member. The investment firm will assess each person for financial reliability, industry reputation, experience relative to the challenges ahead, and the ability to manage a growing business. Most venture capitalists prefer doers to dreamers; says one, "The proven ability to manage a business is as important as having a good idea or business concept."

WOOING WITH FIGURES

Make sure your financial data and projections are substantiated. If you sell countertop cappuccino machines, for instance, you need specific figures showing both the trend from plain coffee to fancy coffee drinks, and the trend toward specialized, home-use, counter-top appliances. Guessing these figures and basing your projections on unsubstantiated estimates will work against you when the venture capitalist company does its due diligence.

In due diligence, the investment firm reviews all your figures, from the amount in your startup bank account to your estimate of the number of people who top their coffee with whipped cream.

Finally, your proposal must show a strong potential for growth that will require a large influx of capital at some point. Venture capitalists are not interested in giving you an amount you could just as easily get from a bank; they are interested in companies that will eventually require at least $1 million. They are risk takers with growth and good profits in mind.

FIVE POINTS FOR TARGETING THE RIGHT INVESTORS

Investment firms are usually interested in ventures of different sizes. Although many private venture capital companies are large institutions and write deals starting in the $5 million range, many others, especially newer companies, target small businesses. Such companies will invest in ventures needing as little as $100,000 with which to finance a startup, while anticipating further investment opportunities as the startup expands and matures.

In order to choose your financial partner wisely, you too must do some investigating. Start by identifying some investment companies. Ask your local business library, entrepreneur's association, accountant and attorney for lists of venture capital companies and, if available, recommendations. Then find the answers to these questions:

1. **Which firms invest in my industry?** Some investment companies are generalists and will look at any venture. Others specialize in specific or related industries, such as medical instruments, hospital supplies, and medical services; or video and audio productions.

2. **Which firms prefer my type of company?** Some investment companies focus on retail, franchise, manufacturing, wholesale, exporting, or service companies.

3. **Which firms look for companies at my company's stage of development?** Some investment companies will accept clients at any stage in their business life; others focus on startups, initial expansion, or mature expansion. Most are interested in new product development.

4. **Which firms are currently investing?** Some investment companies move through cycles from being fully invested to being in an investing mode. Others are always looking for suitable ventures.

5. **Which firms have made investments in the dollar range I need?** Some investment companies will consider ventures of any and every size, others limit themselves to various dollar ranges, such as from $500,000 to $1 million, or from

$1 million to $3 million. Others will only look at investments where another investment company is considering at least a 50 percent investment.

By the time you get the answers to these questions, you should have enough information about each of the firms that could be interested in your company to rank them by their suitability from your perspective. Then approach the most likely company with a succinct letter giving enough information about your venture to interest the investment company in reviewing your portfolio.

Don't make the mistake of mass mailing your business proposal to 100 or more investment firms on the initial list without screening out the least suitable. That approach usually results in a 100 percent rejection, with the possibility of being accepted by the one company you should not do business with! Because you want an investment partner who will relate to your company as the unique opportunity it is, you must seek that partner in an equally individualized manner. It won't take any longer and will cost less money in the long run.

INVEST WITH INTEGRITY

Venture capitalists do more than assess the profit potential of a business venture; they also look at the entrepreneur's integrity, attitudes, track record, and background. When describing the ventures they look for, investors tend to use words like "honorable," "moral," and "ethical" just as often as they use the phrase "high profit potential." This should tell you a lot about the types of ventures, and people, that interest them. It also describes the type of person you should be looking for as an investment partner.

If you select your investment partners carefully, approach them with courtesy and negotiate wisely, you will undoubtedly find people who are as excited about creating your vision as you are.

To start your search, contact the National Association of SBICs which publishes a directory of small-business development companies. (See Appendix C, "Venture Capital.")

CHECKLIST: IS VENTURE CAPITAL RIGHT FOR YOUR BUSINESS?

☐ Do you need more than $500,000 for startup costs?

☐ Will you need regular serial investments of at least $100,000 each to get your product properly launched?

☐ Is your product or concept new, risky, on unproven?

☐ Are you ready for national or international broad-market penetration?

☐ Is your company established and ready for fast growth?

☐ Have you expanded your business plan to meet the venture capitalist's expectations?

☐ Will your business plan stand up to the close scrutiny of the venture capitalist's due diligence?

☐ Do you have an impressive management team?

☐ Can you substantiate your estimates and projections?

☐ How well does this venture capitalist company fit your company's needs?

☐ How well does your firm fit the profile of the company's investment clients?

☐ How important to you are the management, production, sales, and other types of expertise offered by this venture capital company?

☐ What is the worst that could happen and what is the best that could happen under the terms of this venture capital contract?

☐ Is the buyout clause flexible?

14

Seeking Fortune

JOIN A VENTURE CAPITAL CLUB

At the Silicon Valley Entrepreneurs Club in California, the formal presentations don't begin until 10:30 a.m. But when the doors of the connecting ballrooms open at 8:15, the rows of chairs are quickly filled by wide-awake early risers—business owners, inventors, and investors—who have come for the presentation forums. From 8:30 to 10:00 a.m. they listen to advice on writing irresistible business proposals and negotiating with investors.

By the 10:00 a.m. break, the sense of excitement is palpable—an aphrodisiac for financial matings that will result in baby businesses. Then the forum begins. It's simple enough and varies little around the country: Entrepreneurs seeking financing give three- to six-minute presentations on their business concepts and financing needs. Occasionally, someone who wants to join a startup team pitches his or her talents. Only rarely does an investor take the microphone to say publicly what he or she is looking for, but they do jot down names and phone numbers. During the day's breaks, the networking becomes almost frenzied, particularly among the owners of startups and young companies who clutch fistfuls of business cards. Business cards are flourished, displayed to show how much interest is in the holder's concept, yet any card marked with a legitimate investor's encouraging "call me" is tucked safely inside that entrepreneur's wallet.

Even though venture capital clubs don't have any investment funds of their own, they are the fastest-growing trend in
the business financing world. Venture capital clubs bring together entrepreneurs, investment firms, and individual investors or
angels. Most such clubs hold monthly meetings that are attend-
ed by entrepreneurs, inventors, investors, and professionals who
serve the industry, such as accountants, consultants, and attorneys. You never know who you'll sit next to: the person with the
next Pet Rock or Cabbage Patch doll, or someone who makes a
living by connecting great ideas with financiers. On the other
hand, it might be a consultant wanting to earn a good fee cri-
tiquing your business plan, or a representative of one of the leading venture capital companies in the country.

Venture capital clubs are open to anyone with an interest in
finding or providing financing and willing to pay a nominal
membership fee to cover the operational costs. The best of the
clubs present knowledgeable speakers to educate their members
on finding and negotiating the capital contacts they need, and
they structure their meetings to enable good networking.

Venture capital (VC) clubs exist in every state and are
spreading from country to country. Frequently these meetings
are listed in the upcoming events column of the daily newspa-
per. Reference librarians, chambers of commerce, Small Business
Development Centers (SBDCs), and Service Corps of Retired Executives (SCORE) offices usually know which VC clubs are ac-
tive locally. You can also check with state and regional economic development agencies and the business or science
development departments of local universities to find VC clubs
in your area.

VENTURE CAPITAL FAIRS

The second fastest-growing trend in the business world is
probably venture capital fairs. They occur regularly throughout the country. Some are private, organized in conjunction
with trade shows, others are sponsored by state business development departments or universities, often in conjunction
with small-business conferences.

At some fairs investment companies and individual investors are able to rent booths and have their representatives on hand to talk to entrepreneurs and inventors about their proposals and the chances of funding them. Other fairs are organized along the lines of venture capital clubs, in which people looking for financing pitch their products and services to an audience that includes potential investors. The growing trend with venture capital fairs is to screen preregistrants and match them with potential investors by providing private appointments during which entrepreneurs can discuss their funding needs.

Information on venture capital fairs is usually advertised in the business section of newspapers and disseminated to trade associations, local SBDC and SCORE offices, and state and regional departments of commerce and departments of economic development.

DELVE INTO A DATABASE

Venture capital databases have proliferated over the last ten years. The problem is that they vary quite a bit in quality and in the amount of information they offer. Most venture capital databases contain information on both private investors and investment companies, as well as the types of ventures in which they are interested.

Venture capital databases are compiled by private matchmaking companies as well as state departments of commerce, universities, and nonprofit organizations. Some simply provide a list of potential funds for a nominal fee; others are sophisticated enough to match your venture with an appropriate source of funds. Still others are available on disk for you to search yourself. The database operator should be willing to say how frequently, and how recently, the data was updated and verified, because it's not unusual for both individual investors and investment companies to go through cycles when they are fully invested, and you don't want to waste your time contacting people who have not been investing for a year or more.

Companies that provide database matching services are akin to loan brokers. They interview you about your venture and use the database to find a potential investor. They then act as liaison between the entrepreneur and the investor and draw up the investment papers. For these services they take a fee based on the amount of the financing. A good company with a good database can be invaluable, but a poor one will waste your time and is more likely to want an up-front fee for doing a search. These companies are listed in the semiannual International Venture Capital Institute's directory (see Appendix C, "Venture Capital") and should also be listed in your local business telephone directory.

ASK THE PROFESSIONALS

Most SBDC and SCORE offices keep information on local investors and investment companies. In addition, SBDC or SCORE counselors won't charge anything to advise you on how to strengthen your proposal before presenting it to a potential investor. They'll even brief you on whatever they know of the investor's or investment company's preferences.

Another option is to hire an accountant or attorney who specializes in venture capital work. Although these professionals cost a great deal more than SBDC and SCORE counselors, they should do considerably more. These specialists should tell you at the first meeting whether they have clients seeking the type of investment opportunity you are offering and under what circumstances (or with what changes to your package) they would be willing to arrange the introduction or make a presentation on your behalf. Such professionals should be more than counselors; they should be acting as liaison between entrepreneur and investor. If you do use such a professional to find an investor, remember that they probably represent the investor first. You should have your own accountant and attorney take part in any negotiations, and look over any agreement before you sign it.

SURF THE INTERNET

Go for a cruise on the Internet and you'll find the equivalent of venture capital clubs, database matching services, and probably much more. But networking via the Internet is much too new and much too volatile for us to provide directions on how to make contacts. However, since anyone can get on the Internet to find an inventor, startup opportunity, investment opportunity, or money money money, you should heed the advice given under the "Due Diligence" section that follows. We're not trying to scare you off from using a valuable tool; we just want to warn you that you shouldn't let an unknown entity, such as a stranger without a recommendation, control your business, your money, or your life. Be careful.

DO YOUR OWN DUE DILIGENCE

Throughout this book we have pointed out how carefully bankers and investors investigate the proposals they are asked to fund. Presumably you wouldn't put your savings in a bank in which you didn't have confidence, or pick a stock investment by throwing a dart at the NASDAQ index. By the same token, you should protect yourself and your business by investigating any potential investors before accepting their money.

Ask for References

Experienced investors, whether companies or individuals, should be able to provide the names and phone numbers of companies they have worked with that are similar to yours.

Check the References

Ask such questions as the following:

- Is this company similar to yours, in the same stage of development, and so on?
- How easy has it been to work with the investor? Has he or she been available and receptive?
- Were funds available when promised?
- Has the investor made his or her experience available to the management as friendly advice?

- Has the investor tried to dictate how problems should be handled, or has he or she made unreasonable demands?
- How easy were the negotiations? Was the investor willing to work for a win/win contract, or did he or she offer take-it-or-leave-it terms?
- If this investment is over, did the payback go smoothly, without significant problems or demands?
- Would this company use the investor again?

Ask Your Professionals

The counselors at your local SBDC and SCORE offices may know of the investor you are considering or know of companies who have used this investor's financing. Your accountant, attorney, banker, and business consultant may also know about the investor you are considering or be able to find someone who has worked with him or her. The closer you get to signing an agreement with an investor, particularly an investor who is not well known in your own community, the more important it is that you talk with your attorney about making whatever background checks may be appropriate.

Trust Your Experience

By now you should know what personalities you work best with and which you should avoid. Don't let your need for financing override your good sense if your intuition is telling you that a particular investor will be impossible to work with.

No matter how well recommended an investor is, you should remember that your strengths and weaknesses will be thoroughly assessed by that investor, and it's only reasonable that you, too, know your new partner well enough to feel optimistic about your joint venture.

CHECKLIST FOR FINDING VENTURE CAPITAL

☐ Ask for referrals from your accountant, attorney, banker, business consultant, insurance broker, chamber of commerce, or trade association.

☐ Order a directory of SBICs.

☐ Visit SBDC or SCORE, taking your business plan with you.

☐ Call your state department of commerce or business development department.

☐ Check the phone book and local library for regional or local development corporations, venture capital clubs, databases, and venture fairs.

☐ Ask if trade fairs or small-business fairs or conferences will include investor's input, contact, or connecting.

☐ Go on-line and check the Internet for venture capital clubs, database matching services, and investors.

☐ *Be sure to check out the business practices and integrity of those companies you contact.*

15

Back to Basics

By late 1995, Telly Vanes had been marketing his Wonder Water Filtration System on the West Coast for three years, and he was ready to start selling his units in the Midwest. His optimal marketing plan called for an initial investment of $50,000 to duplicate his current method of hiring and training on-the-road sales staff. But Vanes's banker wasn't convinced the Midwest market was strong enough to warrant such an expense. He joked that Vanes needed some "free money."

By mid-January 1996, Vanes had put together an alternate plan to begin testing new markets, and he even had "free" money in the form of a special offer from a major long-distance phone company to finance his new telemarketing efforts.

Vanes knows that purchasing agents are often too busy to meet with his salespeople at the end of the week, so he instructed his on-the-road people to return to Reno on Thursday evenings. Vanes then arranged for them to get in-house telemarketing training through a state-sponsored job-training program at a local college (at considerably less expense than similar training from a corporate employee trainer).

Next he signed up for the long-distance carrier's *Fridays Are Free!* promotion for businesses. Under that plan, any long-distance and overseas calls made from his business on any of the next fifty-two Fridays would be free, provided his other long-distance charges amounted to at least $50 each month. They always did.

By having his salespeople call potential out-of-state customers all day every Friday, and following up the calls with mailed materials, Vanes garnered a steady stream of new orders for his Wonder Water Filtration System. By March, Vanes could justify a four-day out-of-state tour for one sales representative and predicted that by the end of summer he would have the orders and increased income he needed to show his banker that hiring regional representatives was less risky than staying with a single market area.

FINDING FREE MONEY

As you begin estimating the financial needs of your startup business, consider the attractions of "free" money—money you don't have to pay interest on or get in exchange for equity in your business. You need flexibility and innovativeness to find such money, because it can come in many forms, from no- or low-cost training for employees to reliable business counseling that can save sizable sums by avoiding lost time and mistakes. Another source of "free" dollars can be found in your business plan, because every dollar you can shave off your expenses reduces your need to borrow.

Unfortunately, knowing where you can shave your startup costs without creating costly delays often requires more experience than a neophyte entrepreneur has! First-time business owners are at a distinct disadvantage when it comes to projecting costs and cash flow. Even experienced entrepreneurs find it difficult to project exact costs or guess how quickly sales will build. The turbulent waters every business encounters may include unexpectedly high costs that wash away capital, lower sales than anticipated during crucial months, or even a flood of orders that threatens to beach a business by wiping out its cash flow. Not planning for these possibilities is one of the most common reasons businesses fail.

Fortunately, it is possible to add experienced planning to your business plan, by incorporating business assistance into each step of your startup or expansion. With good business counseling you will learn to plan for a range of possibilities, so that when you need that line-of-credit you'll impress your banker with your preparedness. A number of nonprofit organizations will review of your business plan, extend business counseling, and offer classes in management and financial skills. Most of their services are free or cost a nominal amount; some charge on a sliding scale dictated by your business's income.

SCORE WITH VOLUNTEERS

The Service Corps of Retired Executives (SCORE) is sponsored by the Small Business Administration (SBA) and has more than twelve thousand trained volunteers working with small businesses in some seven hundred offices from Maine to Guam, plus in Puerto Rico and the U.S. Virgin Islands. The areas of expertise for SCORE counselors are as varied as the needs you may have, ranging from advertising to banking, credit collection, employee management, financial analysis, importing, manufacturing, merchandising—you get the idea. Whatever your particular problem, your local SCORE office can match you with one or more volunteer retired executives with the experience to advise you.

During your initial visit to a SCORE office, a counselor will review your needs and recommend a plan of action. SCORE stresses a strong business plan so that its clients know exactly what they want to do, know how to get the financing they need, and have every possible chance of either launching a successful business or of turning a less-than-successful business around. Clients who need basic skills are referred to SCORE workshops, which range from business planning to on-line management and are offered at a nominal fee to cover costs.

The next step for most clients is to begin one-on-one counseling which focuses on fine-tuning the business plan, getting financing, identifying problem areas and finding solutions, and identifying weak areas and strengthening them. In-office counseling of this type may last as long as a year and is free.

When it is appropriate for the client, the third step is to match the client with a mentor, who will visit the business whenever needed over the next few years. SCORE mentors, like SCORE counselors, are volunteer retired executives. Mentors are men and women who have elected to work with a limited number of entrepreneurs over an extended time period; their assistance is free.

The caveat in using SCORE counselors is that the organization is run by volunteers, and this strength can become its weakness if you are matched with the wrong person. Neither unqualified approval or rejection are helpful to most of us; we know that our business plans can probably be improved and our strategies refined, and we realize that we don't know all the questions we should ask. A good counselor will point out the flaws in your business plan and suggest how it can be strengthened, and she or he will give fuller answers than your questions require and bring up points you haven't thought of yet.

If you are not getting everything you want from your counselor or mentor, you should definitely broaden your contacts in the SCORE office until you find the right person. However, a SCORE spokesperson warns that "Many entrepreneurs come in to us and say, 'I manufacture shoes, or teakettles, therefore I want someone experienced in the footwear, or teakettle, industry to help me to get into exporting.' Instead they must realize that they are the experts in their industry and the counselor they need is someone with experience where they lack it. True, a consultant with fifty years' experience in exporting heavy equipment won't know all the answers for exporting shoes, but she'll know the export-related steps and the questions to ask that the shoe manufacturer can't even begin to think of.

"Small-business owners also need to realize that it's up to them to keep asking until we get them matched with the right person. If the first or third counselor can't help them and they just drop out we never know why."

From time to time, SCORE gets requests for additional services, which it tries to respond to. For instance, in the last few years women have been starting businesses at six times the rate of men. In response to their requests, SCORE offices have started round-table discussion meetings. These meetings are free, unless the participants have decided to turn them into lunch or dinner meetings. They are structured opportunities for discussion on aspects of entrepreneurialism, so that women can share their experiences with common problems.

In the early 1980s when Magnafish was just a year old, David and Joanne Kelly were forced to admit they really didn't have the expertise they needed to manufacture David's invention. "We build the world's fanciest fish finders," chuckles president Joanne Kelly. The Magnafish is an ultrasonic fish-detecting device that is mounted on the keels of commercial fishing boats. "We needed to learn all aspects of bringing the manufacturing on line," she continues. "We needed a consultant, but when you are a small company, you simply can't afford a consultant's fees."

The Kellys were referred to three SCORE counselors before they found the right person. He began visiting Magnafish regularly to help them design manufacturing procedures for their business. The company now produces a full line of ultrasonic devices and employs nearly thirty people. Joanne and David have continued to draw on the expertise of SCORE volunteers before proceeding with each new phase of Magnafish's development.

"It took time to build a network of SCORE consultants for each aspect of our growth," David Kelly says. "But we could always go back to our key contact and say 'We need to talk to someone who is more—.' With SCORE, you get the expertise of a consultant with years of experience, and it doesn't cost you anything. The people truly have your company's best interests at heart. They are objective, and they give you encouragement. Our company wouldn't be where it is today without their involvement."

BENEFIT FROM SBDCS

Nearly one thousand Small Business Development Centers (SBDCs) are available to help small-business owners. Like SCORE, SBDCs cover a broad geographic area, from Florida to Alaska and from Hawaii to Puerto Rico and the U.S. Virgin Islands. The SBDC's program is financed by a partnership between the SBA and local state governments, with additional contributions from the private sector. Most SBDCs are located in state-run colleges or universities; counseling is free and some workshops have nominal charges to cover expenses.

SBDCs employ business consultants (most with entrepreneurial backgrounds) to teach classes and work with clients individually. This program is the best place to go for information on state and local business requirements, such as how to apply for permits and licenses—they have all the information. But the SBDC's strength is in using community resources—from individuals to banks and trade associations—to supplement their staffs. SBDC counselors are adroit at arranging for a local businessperson to counsel a client for an hour or for a banker to take a second look at a loan application.

The caveat with SBDCs is that you may have to wait for an appointment with a counselor, and most offices simply don't have the resources to have someone visit your business. Unlike a SCORE volunteer who could limit his or her counseling to the needs of a handful of long-term projects, SBDC counselors have to divide their time among the numbers of people requiring assistance. Nevertheless, SBDC assistance is one-on-one when it needs to be.

For example, five years after inheriting Noches Olives, Raoul Noches wanted to expand the family business by adding a pressing plant to manufacture fine olive oil in addition to processed whole and stuffed olives. "I would have given up if it hadn't been for the SBDC," he admits. "Sometimes I got to the point where I figured it would never work, but I'd go back to the SBDC and they would give me more ideas."

Forty-two-year-old Noches tried more than a dozen banks. "As they were closing the door in my face, they would say, 'Well, you have a really good business plan,'" he recalls. "Then I'd go back to my SBDC adviser and she'd say, 'Yes, you have a really good concept and loans are hard to get right now. Keep trying. No, it's not because of your race—I have other clients with plans that are less risky than yours who are having just as difficult a time.' The SBDC people have seen the different sides of the problems you face and have the opportunity and the experience to advise you."

It took five months for Noches to get the $56,000 he needed for the expanded plant and new equipment, but his annual profits have steadily increased and he is now able to provide year-round employment for his workers. "Every time I see our new label I'm reminded that it takes the right sort of assistance, as well as perseverance, to get anywhere," says Noches.

BECOME A WINNER WITH MBDCS

There are approximately one hundred Minority Business Development Centers (MBDCs) serving minority entrepreneurs from New York to Hawaii. Most MBDCs are run by management consulting firms, large accounting firms, university business schools, and state and local government agencies. They focus on providing counseling and management assistance.

MBDC services open with a free hour, which is used to determine what needs the minority-owned company has and how to best meet those needs. This hour could include a brief financial, business, or marketing plan review with both suggestions and referrals to other contacts. Also free is access to a databank of procurement opportunities and registration on a databank of minority procurement providers.

From a service standpoint, MBDCs differ markedly from both SBDCs and SCORE. Rather than teaching and advising small-business owners, they actually work with and for their clients, doing such things as preparing business plans, packaging loan applications and obtaining financing, conducting marketing surveys, and bonding contractors. The fee for these services is remarkably low, just $10 per hour for startups and businesses grossing less than $500,000 annually, and $17.50 per hour for businesses grossing more than $500,000 annually.

When Xavier Quate needed working capital for Unity Metal Stamping, he couldn't understand why his bank kept stalling until he "had some better months." Quate needed working capital to have better months! Finally, Quate turned to the Detroit MBDC for help.

"Together we put together a loan application in the form banks prefer," he says. "I learned what bankers like to see and why, and realized bankers don't know my business, so I had to learn to talk their language. The MBDC helped me think like a banker." Quate got his loan.

SUCCEED WITH WBCD

With the passage of the Women's Business Ownership act of 1988 the Women's Business Center Demonstration (WBCD) project was launched. The WBCD is designed to provide economically disadvantaged women with the skills necessary to launch their own businesses or to run existing businesses successfully.

In 1995, after forty-seven thousand women had benefited from the program, nineteen new sites were opened, bringing the total to fifty-four centers in the rural and urban areas of twenty-eight states. Each site is financed with a partnership of SBA funds and private contributions, and services are free.

The program offers financial, management, marketing, procurement, and technical assistance to women business owners, particularly startups and young companies. As a demonstration program, the centers are able to tailor their programs to the particular needs of their local communities. While SBDC and SCORE offices clearly respond to community needs, these centers can focus in-depth on a single issue. For instance, the National Center for American Indian Enterprise Development in Mesa, Arizona, targets Indian enterprises, the Center for Women & Enterprises, Inc., in Boston, Massachusetts, focuses on women heads of households supporting minor children, and the Foundation for Women's Enterprise in Dallas, Texas, emphasizes training in government contracting opportunities.

FINDING MENTORS AND GETTING TECHNICAL ASSISTANCE

If it is difficult for you to find the time to put together a business plan, or you're just too busy putting out fires to prepare a marketing plan, you will benefit from calling one of these services today. On the other hand, if you are the type of person who does get to the projects that are important but not urgent, you'll benefit most by preparing your business plan, marketing plan, or at least your questions before going in.

If you have a list of questions, try dividing them into three categories:

1. Those that need factual answers, such as "Where can I find out how quickly the sales of countertop kitchen appliances

are growing?" This type of question can be answered by anyone with a knowledge of general business resources.

2. Those that require feedback or advice, such as "After three years in the domestic market and sales of $xxx, should we consider exporting? Is the company ready?" This type of question is better answered by someone with knowledge in your area of concern (in this example, exporting) and preferably with knowledge in your industry. In fact, it's the sort of question you may want to put to as many as three different counselors, both to find a consensus and to get a variety of suggestions on how to proceed. (A consensus may be that all three make similar suggestions of what you need to do, or consider, in coming to your decision.)

3. Those questions that require education and ongoing consulting expertise, such as "We've decided that our product is probably better suited for export than for the domestic market. We need a consultant to point us to the resources for becoming educated in exporting and to advise us on the specific steps as they apply to our business." For this type of question, you want to be matched up with someone who will be

   ▪ Available to work with your company on a long-term basis.

   ▪ Knowledgeable about your area of concern or growth.

To find the SCORE, SBDC, or WBCD office nearest you, look in your local telephone directory under government services, or call the SBA's Answer Desk at (800) 827-5722 or (202) 653-7562. On the toll-free number, a recorded message prompts you to key in information to identify your needs, then answers your questions. Your county library should also have the names and addresses of local business assistance centers, if not at the general reference desk then at the business reference desk. To find your nearest MBDC office, contact the appropriate regional office of the Minority Business Development Agency listed in Appendix B.

Also check with your local colleges, universities, and chambers of commerce, because many of them have excellent small-business programs that include business management and financial counseling. Some college business education departments will even undertake the preparation of a business plan or a market research project at no or nominal cost in order to give their students practical experience.

Plus, whether you need additional financing now or expect to need it in the future, these organizations are usually the first to know who is lending and how to approach those lenders.

FLEXIBLE VIEWPOINT

Are you the type of person who sees the forest, or do you see the trees? Are you great with details, or are you better with the global viewpoint? Or are you somewhere in between?

The most successful entrepreneurs know how to adopt all three viewpoints—they can see how their businesses fit into the national or state marketplace, how their businesses relate to their city's growth or mall's mix, and how they relate to each and every customer.

In financial terms, they know their long-term, medium-term, and short-term needs for both cash and credit. In different financial terms, they know such things as what an optimal marketing plan would cost and what it might reap, how a finance-from-income-only plan compares with the optimal plan, and what they are spending now for what return.

With this breadth of perspective, a small-business owner can address individual financing needs more innovatively. He or she can make the most of the resources available from state, federal, and private agencies as well as commercial entities. And this entrepreneur is never at a loss when it comes to talking up the business with a banker or investor.

CHECKLIST: IS YOUR STARTUP READY TO LAUNCH?

☐ Have you planned a system of records that will keep track of your income and expenses? Will it track what you owe suppliers, as well as what clients and others owe you?

☐ Have you figured a way to track your inventory so that you always have enough on hand for your customers, but not more than you can sell in a reasonable period?

☐ Do you know how to keep payroll records and how to prepare tax reports and payments?

☐ Do you have a cash flow forecast, and have you arranged for income statements and balance sheets to track your progress?

☐ Do you know a bookkeeper and an accountant? The bookkeeper can prepare many of the same records as an accountant, but at a much lower cost; however, the accountant is the person who should do the interpreting.

☐ Do you know what licenses and permits you will need?

☐ Do you know what laws and local regulations you will have to follow?

☐ Do you have a lawyer for advice and help with legal papers?

☐ Have you made a plan for protecting your business against theft (shoplifting, robbery, burglary, employee pilfering)?

☐ Have you discussed this plan with your insurance agent? Have you discussed the kinds of insurance you need?

16

Future Expansion

Innumerable studies have been made to discover why businesses fail. The top two contenders are:

1. Insufficient capital and
2. Inadequate management skills.

In fact, there's a very good chance they are one and the same thing. Inadequate management skills must be the leading cause of starting a business with insufficient capital, and it is undoubtedly why businesses with adequate funds exhaust their money through the inefficient use of available capital. Fortunately, the ingredients of a successful business have been equally well established.

WHAT YOU NEED TO SUCCEED IN BUSINESS

1. A service or product that a customer needs or wants
2. The ability to market the product or service to the consumer
3. The ability to control the cost of production so that you can show an adequate profit when selling the product or service at a price that is acceptable to the consumer

It's a simple, three-point strategy, but it isn't necessarily easy to follow. To effectively use the strategy you also need the following:

1. **A Business Plan.** Essentially, you need a plan based on the loan application package described in Chapter 8, "The Perfect Loan Application," and Chapter 9, "Presenting Your Bottom Line," plus the expansions described in Chapter 3, "Doing Business with a Little Help from Your Friends," and Chapter 13, "Adventures in Financing."

2. **The Ability to Read Financial Statements.** You will need enough expertise at reading financials to control your costs and to understand the seasonal influences, or cycles, affecting your business. At minimum, you should be using a budget and monthly cash flow projections compared to monthly income statements so that you understand the results of your day-to-day decisions in the marketplace.

   Over time, and with your accountant's help, you must acquire the ability to use your balance sheets and income statements to learn how your business is progressing compared to previous years and to similar businesses. You must also acquire the ability to calculate figures such as assets-to-equity and return-on-investment (ROI) ratios and to identify and track your business's individual trends.

3. **A Business Strategy or Strategic Development Plan.** This written document is essentially a continuation of your business plan. Whereas that document describes your business in terms of its past and present, the strategic development plan is the guidebook for taking your business forward to a specific future. Your strategic development plan details your long-term planning and structures your day-to-day operations.

WHY YOU NEED A STRATEGIC DEVELOPMENT PLAN

A strategic development plan will do all of the following:

- Help you to stay ahead of your competition.
- Enable you to predict and prepare for future expenses.
- Force you to think through the consequences of various actions, which will save time and money because you'll act to meet future needs as well as today's demands.
- Clarify your ambitions for your business through the process of writing them down.
- Help you to abandon the "stamping out fires" style of management.
- Facilitate your adopting a "captain at the helm of your ship" management style.
- Clarify where you want to steer your ship. If you don't set goals like "I want to double sales within five years," you will find yourself working for less ambitious, more immediate goals, like meeting payroll or paying taxes on time.
- Provide guidelines for your personnel. When employees can see where the business is going they, too, can commit to taking it there.

THE THREE MILLION-DOLLAR QUESTIONS

Your strategic development plan will eventually document your answers to just three questions:

1. What do I really want to achieve with this business?
2. How can I accomplish that goal?
3. What obstacles must I overcome?

PARTS OF A STRATEGIC DEVELOPMENT PLAN

1. Introduction
2. Mission statement
3. Analysis of competition

4. Market niche
5. Assessment of profit potential
6. Assessment of obstacles and advantages
7. Identification of goals and time frames
8. Steps for implementing strategy
9. Performance review

PREPARING THE STRATEGIC DEVELOPMENT PLAN

If you hope to prepare a practical, rather than an ideal but unrealistic, plan you should involve your employees, advisors, partners, mentors and spouse in the plan's preparation. A working group of four or five people seems optimal for bouncing ideas, giving feedback, and asking leading questions. Later, bring in other people to individually review the plan and make suggestions as it develops.

As you work together, everyone should be charged with the task of constantly looking for those attributes that make this business different or better, and that set it apart from the competition—the element that gives it positive visibility in the community. You are looking for the ingredient that will become the *flair* you will use to present your product or service, and it will be the element that is hardest for your competition to copy.

Introduction

This written statement of the values that will guide your company describes the basic philosophy behind all your management decisions. It is this philosophy that makes your company unique in the eyes of your employees, your customers and the community. Cover such topics as the following:

1. **How We Treat Customers.** What you offer your customers will dictate the basis of their loyalty. Will they come to you for low prices, community involvement, high quality, extra service, or something else? Whatever it is, it should be so much a part of your business's identity that it will continue in all

circumstances and conditions. Loyal customers can see you through a recession when nothing else will.

2. **How We Treat Employees.** Keeping good employees depends on much more than money and benefits. Good employees look for qualities and activities such as participative goal setting, job satisfaction, skills advancement, job enrichment, participation in decisions, community recognition of their company, quality communication, teamwork, fair treatment, and feeling appreciated.

3. **How We Treat Suppliers.** If your suppliers appreciate doing business with you (not just the business you give them for its dollar value), they will go the extra mile for you whenever they see the need. Ask yourself which of your suppliers would be most likely to respond with a firm "yes" when you ask for that special favor, such as extra credit or an overnight shipment.

4. **How We Are Viewed in the Community.** Your business is part of a series of entities. From a location perspective, there's the mall or street in which you are situated, your town, your region, your state, and the country. From an industry perspective, there's the perception of your industry held by the public, the government regulations or standards it upholds, and the local and national trade associations. In each of these venues you can act to improve the business climate for all businesses and see your own business rewarded.

5. **How We Meet Our Responsibilities.** Your lenders and investors will look to you for regular reports on the progress of your business, particularly as it concerns their interests. Since future expansion will most likely depend on the goodwill of these same people, ensuring their continued support is important.

You may also have responsibilities to other people or institutions who have an interest in the success of your business, including your professional associates and associations, and any local, state, or federal regulators.

Mission Statement

This written statement of the intent of your company should be a clear, concise guide for deciding what products and services you will offer to which markets. The mission statement must result from the process of working through the preparation of your business strategy, because it reflects that combination of product or service and the market niche where your business has special capabilities or a unique advantage. Your mission statement describes your business not as what it will become, but *as what it strives to be each day.*

Analysis of Competition

By analyzing the competition, you will be able to direct your marketing efforts where they will be most effective. Answer these questions:

1. Who is your competition?
2. What are their strengths and how does your business compare with those strengths?
3. What are their weaknesses and how does your business compare in this area?

An analysis of your competition and your comparative strengths and weaknesses should reveal the one or two areas in which you have the greatest advantage. The most important areas of advantage are price/cost, quality, and customer service. Part of your philosophy should be to capitalize on your strengths, while improving your weaknesses.

Market Niche

Knowing your market niche helps you to focus your business, so that you are not trying to do, or sell, everything to everybody. Answer these two basic questions:

1. What type of products or services will your business provide?
2. What types of customers or markets will your business serve?

The answers to those two questions should be framed in terms of how you define your business—your business orientation. For instance, if you see your business as providing a product or service based on specialized knowledge (an expertise orientation), you will answer one way; if the product or service you offer is the core of your business (a product orientation), you will answer another way; and if the markets or customers you serve are central to your efforts (a market orientation), you will answer a third way. The great benefit of defining your business by its orientation is that it allows you to do one thing very well indeed, instead of several things incompletely. Note the following examples:

Market Orientation. When the first voice-entry computer systems were developed, they were targeted at doctors who used medical terminology in clinic and hospital settings. All of that company's research, development, and marketing efforts were directed to serving those clients. Such an approach could have included auxiliary products enabling voice entry onto commonly used forms, or enabling a doctor to dictate certain notes and a medical typist to complete the records. A market orientation is right for the company that will endeavor to meet the needs, however broad, of a specific market; the products or services may vary widely.

Product Orientation. By 1995, IBM dominated voice-entry computer systems products, and the company appears to have oriented its research, development, and marketing to product development and dissemination. IBM seems to be concentrating on improving the basic product, which it is marketing to anyone and everyone who expresses interest. A product or service orientation is right for the company that will market specific products or services to every segment of the market.

Expertise Orientation. Meanwhile, a number of companies have been launched from the basis of having a body of knowledge. When Ron Katsuranis, a computer consultant in Belmont, California, began VoiceWare Systems, he defined his area of expertise as providing "voice-entry dictation systems for those who don't know how to type." "Two things happened to make me change this approach," says Katsuranis. "First, I realized that there was an equally large client base among people who knew how to type but because of repetitive motion disorders could not do so. Second, I found other products for these people." Katsura-nis now defines his marketable product as his expertise in installing customized computer-entry systems. His physical products include systems for voice entry, specialized mouse units, and programmed foot pedals, and his business can expand as new products are developed. His client base now includes nontypists, such as doctors, attorneys, and scientists (all with specialized vocabularies), and people in a multitude of professions whose injuries prevent them from typing; he also installs systems for corporations seeking ergonomic solutions to heavy keyboarding. An expertise orientation may be translated into multiple products or services for multiple markets, but it will always stem from a body of knowledge that is the company's principal asset.

Although there are other possible business orientations, these are the three most common. To decide which orientation best fits your company's mission, weigh your answers to the following questions:

1. Which approach to defining our business will give us the fewest competitors?
2. Which approach to defining our business will give us the broadest base of potential customers?
3. Which approach to defining our business will be the least vulnerable to sudden changes in forces beyond our control, such as economic, social, or political conditions?
4. Which approach to defining our business best utilizes the skills, knowledge, production capability, research and development, marketing expertise, sales ability, and other attributes that we either have or can most easily acquire?
5. Which approach to defining our business can be undertaken with the economic resources we have available and with the least increase in our debt load?

Assessment of Profit Potential

The financial section of your strategic development plan is the acid test for the other sections. The figures you pull together here will be based on the decisions made in those areas and if the numbers don't result in a steady and adequate cash flow, a profit, and an adequate return on your investment, then you need to rethink the earlier assumptions.

Assessment of profit potential must start with pulling together as much information as possible on the market niche you intend to target and the potential for sales of your product or service. You may have to undertake specific market research to get the information necessary to make reasonably reliable sales projections.

Your assessment of profit must include a time line for paying off your indebtedness and possibly for buying out any investors. Chapter 17, "Planning for Long-Term Capital Expenses," will help you to pull this information together.

Assessment of Obstacles and Advantages

An ongoing assessment of the obstacles and advantages confronting your business will enable you to overcome the first while recognizing and utilizing the second.

Start by identifying the capabilities or assets you need to maintain or acquire within your own resources; consider human resources, financial resources, technological resources, and those resources that are specific to your industry and business.

Identification of Goals and Time Frames

This section details the master strategies you choose and the specific tactics you adopt to make the most of opportunities and guard against threats. This section, in combination with your mission statement, breathes life into your document and moves you from reacting to the marketplace and what your competition is doing to setting your own direction. Goals are most successful when they are challenging yet attainable, specific, and measurable. They save time and money by directing effort where it will do the most to further the company's mission. You should list the actions to be taken quite specifically:

- State what you and each of your employees will do.
- State when you and each of your employees will act.
- State each goal so that its accomplishment can be measured.

Steps for Implementing Strategy

Strategy steps should be spelled out as separate items from the goals. Again, you will focus on specific factors:

- Identifying what you and each of your employees will do.
- Identifying when you and each of your employees will act.

Performance Review

Your performance review is a vital part of your strategic development plan. It's not only where you adjust the figures and dates because you find that more, or less, progress is possible than you estimated; it's your essential training to improve your ability to estimate what your business can do in various conditions over a period of time. Ask yourself these key questions:

1. Is the project on track? If not, why not? What needs to be changed?
2. Is the project generating the expected results or returns? If not, why not? What needs to be changed?

FINAL TIPS

- See the next chapter for advice on developing the financial section of your strategic development plan.
- Include a goal for how frequently you will review the plan.

No business can remain static—it either grows or diminishes. Therefore, as you achieve some goals, you must set new ones.

Moreover, over the long term the philosophies of both individuals and societies evolve, and your plan must reflect this evolution. We have only to look back at the business philosophy our parents might have written to recognize that ten years from now even the most forward-thinking strategic development plan will show signs of changing.

CHECKLIST: WHAT IS THE STRATEGIC DEVELOPMENT PLAN FOR YOUR BUSINESS?

Describe the parts of a strategic development plan, both in general terms and with notes on what issues have to be considered in your business.

- ☐ Introduction
    - ☐ Customers
    - ☐ Employees
    - ☐ Suppliers
    - ☐ Community
    - ☐ Responsibilities
- ☐ Mission statement
- ☐ Analysis of competition
    - ☐ Strengths
    - ☐ Weaknesses
- ☐ Market niche
    - ☐ Market orientation
    - ☐ Product orientation
    - ☐ Expertise orientation
- ☐ Assessment of profit potential
- ☐ Assessment of obstacles and advantages
- ☐ Identification of goals and time frames
- ☐ Steps for implementing strategy
- ☐ Performance review

17

Planning for Long-Term Capital Expenses

An essential part of your strategic development plan is your budgeting for long-term capital expenses. By their nature, capital expenses require relatively large amounts of money, and if not planned for they can become crisis purchases. For instance, when do you usually replace your primary family automobile?

1. When the cost of repairs is more than the vehicle is worth?
2. When you get a raise, land a big contract, or have the money?
3. When you deserve a new car?
4. When it has xxx miles on it, anticipated at 199x?

Unless you selected number 4, you have an attitude toward capital expenses that could be very costly to your business.

IS YOUR IMAGE IN PLACE?

Paint gets dingy, and when a business's image becomes tired and worn it invites the competition to move in. In 1990 a major drugstore chain opened a new store in a small coastal town in northern California and the other national chain, the one that had been in that town for twenty years, suddenly found itself with nobody in its aisles. Within weeks, the latter chain was drawing up plans to remodel (and to fill the shelves twice weekly instead of once monthly) in order to effect a comeback. Said the manager, "If we had spent half this money two years ago we might not be sharing our local customer base with our largest national competitor today!"

Take a look at your facilities, particularly those that convey your image to your customers:

- How often should the walls be painted?
- How often should the floors be recovered?
- How often should the fittings be spruced up or replaced?
- What do your delivery trucks look like?
- Are your logo, your stationary, and your forms reflecting your current image?

ARE YOUR WORKERS PRODUCTIVE?

Next, take a look at the environment where your employees work. True, most expenses here can be delayed if necessary; but no, it's not true that they are not necessary.

- Are work areas clean, bright, and hazard free? Injuries and allergies can keep employees away from work.
- Is the lighting good: adequate brightness, without glare or casting shadows across work areas? Eyestrain and headaches can slow production, cause mistakes, and negatively affect how your employees relate to customers.
- Do workers have adequate storage and work surfaces? Clutter, especially piles of boxes or files, mean time is being lost while searching for misplaced items and from scrunched working conditions.

- Is the work area cheerful and inviting? Dingy offices are very effective in discouraging good work habits.

- Do chair backs support the body, are keyboards at the right height, are telephones within reach? Discomfort can cause tardiness, absenteeism, excessive water cooler activity, and low employee morale. Cheerful, comfortable surroundings have proven their value in higher productivity and better service to customers.

LONG-TERM CAPITAL EXPENSES

Long-term capital expenses can be divided into three categories. Which category takes priority at any given time depends on your mission statement and the business philosophy on which it is based, as well as the available capital and the time demands of specific items.

- The first category covers the expenses necessary for business growth.

- The second category involves the expenses necessary to maintain your competitive edge.

- The third category includes purchases beyond your control. If, for instance, you have to make changes in your facilities or operation because of state, Occupational Safety and Health Administration (OSHA), or Environmental Protection Agency (EPA) regulations you may not have the option to schedule them at a convenient time. However, if your industry is being discussed by any regulatory body, you can plan for possible expenditures. If they don't materialize, or are less costly than anticipated, you will have money on hand for preferred expenses. At worst, you'll be able to show your banker that you began planning for the crisis as early as possible.

Your strategic development plan should always be treated as a working document, with periodic revisions; but the long-term capital expense is the one section that should definitely be scheduled for annual review.

As you work through the questions in this chapter, draw up a list of future expenses with estimated costs and time frames. You will enter this information into a long-term budgeting forecast.

CAPITAL EXPENSES FOR BUSINESS GROWTH

Businesses grow by increasing their market shares, finding new markets, and bringing in new products and services. They also grow by dropping products and services, and markets, that are no longer profitable, thereby freeing up time and space for more profitable endeavors.

Obviously, businesses vary greatly, and we can only give very general guidelines for discovering and listing the expenses that you will incur from growing your business, especially from growing your business in new or auxiliary directions. But essentially there are two sets of questions:

What budget is appropriate over what long-term period to take my business from its present volume to the maximum it can handle in its current facility with current major equipment?	What time and dollar budget will I need to expand our facilities, purchase new equipment, hire additional staff, and begin a new stage of growth?

Consider the following topics as you answer these questions:

- New products and services
- Additional equipment to add products
- Advertising and promotion to expand markets or launch new products
- Additional staff: professional, sales, office, manufacturing, warehouse
- Expanded distribution: delivery fleet versus outside distributors, exporting
- Additional facilities: retail outlets, regional offices, specialized manufacturing plants

- New facilities for retailing, manufacturing, administration, warehousing

If yours is a new business, the second question may be answered some time in the future—right now you're planning to have your business survive its first months and become a viable concern as quickly as possible. But for either a startup or a mature business to grow, it does need a plan. Consider the example of Yukon-Zanzibar Tours.

"There are lots of tours offered to the Yukon," explains Katrina Jansen, "so we called our company Yukon-Zanzibar Tours because we knew from the beginning that we wanted to run exotic tours all over the world, not just in Canada."

"We started with a good business plan," adds her sister, Aida, "because we were able to draw on the plans of the two companies we'd worked for."

When the sisters entered the touring industry in the early 1980s, they had no intention of eventually starting a company together—they just wanted to work overseas and see the world. But in 1987, when their parents were killed in an auto accident and they both returned to British Columbia, they had to assess their assets.

"We inherited three touring buses, which were leased to other companies, and a house. Since we were experienced in different aspects of running bus tours, we decided not to renew the leases as they expired, and to take a second mortgage on the house to launch our own company," says Katrina.

"We were really very fortunate," adds Aida. "Launching the business helped us to keep going during a traumatic time, and we had some excellent family expertise providing advice and hands-on assistance. But after five years we were getting frustrated because we couldn't see our business expanding overseas, and we both had itchy feet."

"We hadn't realized that if you don't plan for something like that, it just doesn't happen. The business just doesn't seem to generate the capital needed, and we were too busy with day-to-day operations anyway."

"But we finally got the word and started to put together a strategic development plan."

"It really made us rethink what we wanted for our business and our lives. We realized we had grown Yukon-Zanzibar Tours with the easy-market, comfy-travel type tours we'd worked for rather than the exotic, adventure-style tours we'd dreamed about!"

The process of refocusing their goals meant redirecting their company, but these two women immediately began budgeting for the equipment they would need for overseas adventure tours, and they took turns researching their first non-Canadian ventures. This year they will be offering their first overseas adventure tour, to Ayres Rock and Kakadu National Park in Australia. "We drew straws to see who would lead this first adventure tour," says Aida, "and Katrina won! But that's okay because we're both really excited about our new direction, and know it wouldn't have happened if we hadn't gone through the last three years of planning and financing, tough though they were."

Alternatively, you might never want to be larger than a single store or a business that provides personalized services from owner to client with minimal support staff. The questions listed previously are not meant to suggest that you should do anything other than work toward your own goals. But the desire to remain small doesn't preclude the need for strategic planning, which can be used effectively to grow or to limit growth to what you're comfortable with while ensuring that you are spending your time on the projects that interest you most.

STRATEGIC PLANNING WITHOUT GROWTH

Danielle Villanueva says, "I started an interior design business intending to specialize in clients who were moving from large homes to inner-city apartments, mostly upscale empty-nesters. Problem was that in the first three years I took any and all jobs just to get going, and found myself with a reputation for getting first-time homeowners economically installed—which wasn't earning me the commissions I needed!

"At a time when I really felt like abandoning an apparently successful business because of my own burnout, I needed to take time away to think things through." Villanueva visited a Small Business Development Center (SBDC) counselor who pointed out that she needed a business strategy to redirect her efforts. "I almost refused, because it seemed so much like starting all over again!"

Within twelve months of completing her strategic development plan, Villanueva had redirected her business and was working extensively with the artists and artisans whose creativity had attracted her into the business. "I'll never have more than one or two part-time employees, but now I'm putting work with creative people who need the outlet I provide," reports an elated Villanueva.

CREATING A SCHEDULE OF CAPITAL EXPENSES

Debt to finance major capital expenditures is a demand against future earnings and the fewer such demands you incur for foreseeable expenses, the more resources you will have to respond to opportunities. At least once each year you should review your entire business to update your schedule of capital expenses. This schedule of capital expenses should include time and dollar estimates for major maintenance, upgrading, or replacements in seven major areas. As you review each area, consider its impact on your image with customers, your ability to provide service, your productivity, and—last but certainly not least—the safety of your customers and your employees.

1. **Facilities That Convey Your Image:** storefront, shop interior, location advertising, and so forth.
2. **Employee Environment:** such as warehouse, offices, kitchens, grounds, and location.
3. **Rolling Stock:** cars, delivery trucks, and so forth.
4. **Equipment and Machinery:** Compare life expectancy with greater productivity from upgrades. If you don't plan to replace equipment as it reaches its life span, and upgrade machinery when new products offer productivity gains, then you are planning to let your competitor serve your customers better than you can.

5. **Computer Systems:** accounting, order handling, inventory, specialized uses. How well is the system handling what it needs to do? How well will it handle growing or changing demands? How much more productive could it be?

6. **Inventory Systems, Communication Systems, and Specialty Systems:** Are they operating optimally for your business or industry?

7. **Staff Training:** The demands of some industries change rapidly and dictate continuous training, and regulators of some industries require practitioners to acquire new learning on an annual basis, but all businesses benefit from some type of staff training on a regular basis. Staff training could be directed to upgrading job skills, handling new equipment, or instituting a companywide policy of quality control or customer service.

PLANNED LIQUIDITY

As part of both your short- and long-term financial planning, you should include a policy of cash on hand. How much liquidity your business needs will depend greatly on the variants of your business cycle and the average time it takes to collect your receivables. There are various rules of thumb for deciding how much cash to have on hand:

- The equivalent of three months' expenses;
- The equivalent of the expenses for one full business cycle (for example, if you have two main sales seasons, in November-December and July-August, you would have six-month business cycles);
- The equivalent of the cash needed for your most "expensive" period, that is, the period when you are building inventory for seasonal demand.

If you are putting aside a monthly amount toward long-term maintenance, upgrading, and replacement, you have a built-in cushion for when operating capital is being stretched.

Long-term reserve amounts should be kept in your bank's certificates of deposit or other fixed deposit accounts where they are optimal vehicles for line-of-credit collateral. Long-term reserve accounts can also recommend your creditability by providing a record of:

1. Reliability of regular, timely deposits
2. Reputation for planning for foreseeable expenses
3. Establishment of your business as a good customer that uses the services that allow the bank to make a profit
4. A healthy cash-to-debt ratio, even if your operating account is running low

THE LONG-TERM CASH-FLOW FORECAST

The pivotal document in your Strategic Development Plan is your Long-Term Cash-Flow Forecast. It will show you how much you want in your reserve account to minimize borrowing, and it will enable you to schedule downtime when it has the least effect on your business's productivity.

Begin by preparing a cash-flow sheet that includes all the major expenses you have indentified so far. Depending on your business, long-term could be five years, fifteen years, or twenty-five years. Select the time span that fits your longest-term major expenses, and use a column sheet like the samples shown on pages 184 and 185. Enter the purchase items in the left-hand column, and project the estimated costs in the relevant time columns. Most probably you will have groups of expenses in some time frames and no expenses in others. Move things around until you are satisfied that product and market additions are made according to your goals, that major maintenance will be performed in a timely manner, and that replacements and upgrades will occur as they are needed. Check the "Goals and Time Frames" section of your business development strategy and add any items that did not come up in this financial review. You will also want to integrate this section into the rest of your business development strategy document as you complete the time-dollar budget.

Five-Year Long-Term Cash-Flow Budget

Expense Items	1996				1997	1998	1999	2000
	1st qtr	2nd qtr	3rd qtr	4th qtr				
Awnings		5000						5000
Expanded loading dock							15000	
Delivery trucks					12000			12000

Fifteen-Year Long-Term Cash-Flow Budget

Expense Items	1996	1997	1998	1999	2000	2001-5	2006-10	2011-15
1. Facilities/ image								
Awnings	5000					5000	5000	5000
2. Facilities/ production								
Expanded loading dock			15000					
Second loading dock							25000	
3. Rolling stock								
Delivery trucks	12000		13000			27000	29000	30000

Twenty-Five-Year Long-Term Cash-Flow Budget

	1996-2000	2001-2005	2006-2010	2011-2015	2016-2020
Projected totals:	$45,000	$50,000	$48,000	$70,000	$50,000
Cumulative totals:	$45,000	$95,000	$143,000	$213,000	$263,000
Average cost for each of five years in each time frame:	$9,000	$10,000	$9,600	$14,000	$10,000
Average annual deposit to meet each total by the final year of its time frame:	$9,000	$9,500	$9,534	$10,650	$10,520

Use a cumulative sheet from 1996 to 2020 in five-year columns, plus separate sheets for the next five years.

This is the simplest way of figuring how much must be set aside each year to meet long-term capital expenses. If this company elects to pay for each five-year's projected expenses within the time frames in which they are needed, its annual capital outlays will vary from $9,000 to $14,000. However, as the "average annual deposit" item shows, the strain on the higher-cost years could be relieved by increasing the amount annually set aside from the $9,000 required in each of the first five years by just $1,650, to $10,650 per year. It also shows that if the company has a short fall and only averages an annual deposit in its **Long-Term Capital Expense account** of $10,520, the additional amounts needed in 2011-2015 could be financed over the next five years.

Suppose, however, that the projected totals equaled amounts far greater than this company is able to put aside in its early years; the budget forecast would then alert management to the need to look for alternate financing in the form of new equity or capital-expense loans.

The next step is to use this information to estimate the amounts that need to be invested in a Long-Term Capital Expenses account each year. In the "Steps for Implementing Strategy" section of your strategic development plan, include a schedule for making regular deposits in your Long-Term Capital Expenses account. Some businesses benefit from monthly deposits in this account, others need to be structured quarterly, half-yearly, or annually. Determine how frequently you should make your deposits by examining your annual cash-flow budget. Actually, it's less important that deposits be made frequently than that they be made regularly. To a banker, the evidence of such regular deposits shows that you have the self-discipline required for paying off a loan. Nevertheless, your planning needs to be flexible since good years will enable you to get ahead of your schedule and more easily handle a year when you cannot invest the full amount.

ACTING WITH DOLLARS

Having done the hard work, executing the long-term budget should be easy. Well, at least on the spending side!

When it comes time to review the projected capital expenses for the current year, you'll need to compare what's wanted with the capital on hand and the credit available and prioritize according to your needs, timing, and financial resources. Fortunately, there are guidelines for deciding when to use your cash and when to arrange financing:

1. Perhaps the most basic guideline is the principle of only financing that which generates profit that is greater than the cost of the financing; question the necessity for everything else or delay those purchases until the cash is available.

2. As some expenses will generate the income that can be used to finance their purchase, it doesn't make sense to delay getting a more efficient piece of equipment if your market will absorb the additional volume and the additional revenues will pay for the equipment within a reasonable amount of time.

3. It may be necessary to evaluate competing expenditures to decide which should have priority. One way to do this is to calculate how long it will take the equipment, for example, to

pay for itself. To figure this, divide the total investment by the total annual return plus the annual depreciation of the capital investment.

When Xavier Quate, owner of Unity Metal Stamping in Detroit, had to decide between purchasing a milling machine and a stamping machine, he compared them as follows:

		Milling machine	Stamping machine
A.	Total investment cost	$6,000	$6,000
	Equipment life	5 years	10 years
	Average annual depreciation	$1,200	$ 600
	Average annual return	$1,800	$2,000
B.	Total annual return and depreciation	$3,000	$2,600
C.	Years to pay back (A/B = C)	2 years	2.3 years

As Quate's calculations show, the stamping machine would yield a higher average annual return, the milling machine would yield higher depreciation, and for the same outlay the milling machine would provide a faster return on capital. In this example, the "total investment cost" would include the cost of financing if Quate was not paying cash.

4. Quate could also make his comparison based on average return on investment, which would allow him to assess the yield from each piece of equipment. Average return on investment is figured by dividing the average annual savings or return by half of the net investment outlay.

		Milling machine	Stamping machine
	Total investment cost	$6,000	$6,000
A.	Half of total investment cost	$3,000	$3,000
	Equipment life	5 years	10 years
	Average annual depreciation	$1,200	$ 600
B.	Average annual return	$1,800	$2,000
	Total annual return and depreciation	$3,000	$2,600
C.	Average return on investment (B/A = C)	60%	66.6%

This method of comparison shows that the stamping machine would provide a higher average return than would the milling machine, and financially it would be a more attractive investment.

5. There are other methods of comparing the cost and value of capital expenditures that have multiple variables. Unless you need to make such calculations frequently, in which case a good text on financing equations would be worth studying, your accountant can help you select and make the most appropriate calculations. Obviously, any capital expense cannot be made strictly according to the figures, because some benefits are intangible. How, for instance, do you calculate a return, yield, or savings on periodically repapering your restaurant's walls and recarpeting the floor? Yet unless the restaurant maintains its image, it will gradually cease to attract its clientele.

As part of establishing good relationships with your banker and your angels, we recommend that you discuss the financial parts of your strategic development plan with them. They undoubtedly have experience that can benefit you, and they will appreciate being kept informed of your plans. Bankers, in particular, take a positive view of clients who plan for foreseeable expenses and make arrangements for adequate cash reserves well in advance of need.

18

The Final Equation

There's just one more ratio you need to know how to figure and just one more evaluation you need to know how to make. The ratio is return on investment, or ROI. The evaluation is what your business is worth to you.

FIGURING ROI

Return on investment is a term you'll hear from bankers, angels, venture capitalists, and just about anyone in the business world. It's a bottom-line computation. It's easy to figure, it can provide a clear basis for comparison, and it can be overused.

ROI is figured by dividing the income from the investment by the principal (or amount invested). Thus:

$482.66 / $10,000 = 4.826% return
$1,000 / $10,000 = 10% return
$1,666 / $10,000 = 16.66% return

When your banker makes a loan to your business of $10,000 at 9 percent interest over three years, with monthly installments of principal and interest, the bank will receive:

36 installments of $318 = $11,448 or $3,816 each year

- The first year the bank will receive $776.66 in interest and $3,039.34 in principal. The $776.66 interest represents a 7.76 percent return on the $10,000 loaned at the beginning of the year.

- The second year the bank will receive $491.55 in interest and $3,324.45 in principal. The $491.55 interest represents a 7.06 percent return on the $6,960.66 outstanding at the beginning of the year.

- The third year the bank will receive $179.79 in interest and $3,636.21 in principal. The $179.79 interest represents a 4.94 percent return on the $3,636.21 outstanding at the beginning of the year.

When your brother invests $10,000 in the stock market, and at the end of three years sells his stock for $13,000, he will receive $3,000 income, which equals $1,000 per year, or a return on the total investment of 10 percent per year.

If your brother becomes your angel and invests the $10,000 in your business for three years, the business may do so well that you pay him a dividend of $1,000 at the end of the first and second years and buy back his equity for $13,000 at the end of the third year. Your angel will receive $5,000 income, which equals $1,666 per year, or a return on the total investment of 16.66 percent per year.

When Xavier Quate, owner of Unity Metal Stamping in Detroit, invests $6,000 in a milling machine and receives a total annual return (with depreciation) of $3,000 per year, he receives:

$$\$3,000 / \$6,000 = 50\%$$

a return on the total investment of 50 percent per year

When Xavier Quate invests $6,000 in a stamping machine and receives an annual return (with depreciation) of $2,600 per year, he receives:

$$\$2,600 / \$6,000 = 43.33\%$$

a return on the total investment of 43.33 percent per year

ROI as a Trend

Back in Chapter 9, "Presenting Your Bottom Line," we described how Sourpuss figured ROI as a trend showing the increased value of her business. To figure ROI as a trend, divide the net worth on each year's balance sheet by the previous year's net worth, because the current net worth represents the annual increase (or decrease) from the capital in the business at the end of the previous year. By figuring ROI for several consecutive years, you can see whether your business is increasing, maintaining, or decreasing its return.

Figuring ROI on Your Business

A simpler way to figure ROI on your business is to divide the current worth of your business by the capital you invested. If your business has a book value of $100,000 today, and you started it ten years ago with a $40,000 initial investment, the ten-year ROI would be 150 percent, equaling 15 percent per year average.

$$\$60,000 / \$40,000 = 150\% / 10 \text{ (years)} = 15\%$$
$$\text{or } \$6,000 / \$40,000 = 15\%$$

But suppose you have drawn each year's profit as your income? After all, some businesses don't require very much in the way of capital investments and have little inventory. What's being sold is a service, or the product is of a knowledge orientation. Many home-based businesses fall into this category, even when they have employees. Yes, you can still figure your ROI and it still makes sense to do so periodically as a measure of your business's success.

1. First you need to figure out how much you have invested in equipment. In a home office this could be your furniture, computers and printers, fax, photocopier, telephone systems, and so on. Add in an estimate for the supplies you usually have on hand and, depending on the nature of your business, you might also include such expenses as the cost of a recent major advertising campaign. Then add the average value of whatever inventory you carry.

2. Next, from the amount you have drawn in the past twelve months deduct the amount you might reasonably expect in

salary if you were employed in a corporation. The difference is the income from your investment.

3. Divide this investment income amount by the total of your investment for your ROI. If you figure this on an annual basis, it will very quickly tell you when you should be raising your fees.

Total drawn in 1995:	$75,000
Comparable salary:	$60,000
Investment income:	$15,000
Value on hand:	$20,000

$15,000 / $20,000 = 75%

If instead you divided your total income for 1995 by the value of your business you would have an equation of

$$\$75,000 / \$20,000 = 375\%$$

return on your value and would have worked for nothing. But that's not a very practical way to assess your business.

FIGURING THE WORTH OF YOUR BUSINESS

There are many way to figure the worth of your business, depending on why you wish to do so.

If the business is being offered for sale, its equipment is assessed differently than the depreciated book value, because depreciated book value is a tax configuration and doesn't represent either what the equipment is worth on the secondhand market or to an operating business. Moreover, a seller wants to justify the highest price possible. On the other hand, if the business is being valued for inheritance taxes, everyone but the government wants it valued at the lowest price possible.

Some say that valuing a business is an art rather than a science, and others are adamant that ROI is the only logical way to go; they point out that if you had the value of your business as cash, you could invest it in the stock market at a certain(?) 10 percent.

While it's not unreasonable to expect a return on your capital in addition to your "salary," the next time someone suggests that business A is a better business because it has a higher ROI than business B, you might point out that if business B's owner takes the value of the business and puts it in the stock market, then he or she will be out of work.

Two friends lunching together came to just that conclusion recently. Five years ago, they left comparable corporate positions to start businesses based on retail sales. Linda Chan used $10,000 of her savings to start a home-based business, which has given her the overseas travel she wanted, a new car every second year, and a higher salary than she was making. Patricia Wu used $75,000 of home equity to open a retail store. She hasn't bought a new car, but has enjoyed two overseas vacations. Patricia Wu draws more salary than Linda Chan, but they both draw more than they would if managing comparable businesses. So who has the better business?

Linda Chan figures her office equipment and inventory are worth about $15,000. She drew $60,000 last year, and the business paid $20,000 for her latest car. Her corporate salary was $50,000 a year.

Linda Chan's total income:	$80,000
Less her corporate salary:	$50,000
Investment income:	$30,000
Current total investment:	$15,000
$30,000/$15,000 = 200% return	

Patricia Wu has a net worth in her business of $80,000. She drew $65,000 last year, and the business paid the final 20 percent off the home equity loan she used for startup funding. Those payments amounted to just under $18,250. She's still driving the same car, and her corporate salary was also $50,000 a year.

Patricia Wu's total income:	$83,250
Less her corporate salary:	$50,000
Investment income:	$33,250
Current total investment:	$80,000
$33,250/$80,000 = 42% return	

So despite the similarity in what each woman draws from her business, Linda Chan's business is producing a return on equity of more than four times what Patricia Wu's business is doing. Does that make it a better investment? If both women were hospitalized, Patricia Wu's business could be run by a manager; it's less vulnerable.

But Linda Chan only has $15,000 tied up in her business. She'd lose less if she experienced a disaster that put her out of business. On the other hand, if Patricia Wu is ever disabled she would have a salable concern, which Linda Chan does not.

The point of this discussion is that ratios, velocity of profit growth, and business worth are minor elements when compared with the satisfaction of being in business for yourself in order to create a business entity and a lifestyle that suits you to a T.

Yes, you should learn to use every tool there is, operate your business with integrity, and create something unique. That's the true recipe for getting the financing you need to make your dream come true.

Small-Business Development Centers

Each of the fifty-six Small Business Development Centers listed here has one or more satellite SBDC offices providing one-on-one counseling, information on licenses, regulations, financing, and other services, and holds workshops or classes for local entrepreneurs.

Alabama
    SBDC, University of Alabama
    1717 11th Avenue South, #419
    Birmingham, AL 35294
    205/934-7260, fax/934-7645

Alaska
    SBDC, University of
    Alaska/Anchorage
    430 West 7th Ave., #110
    Anchorage, AK 99501
    907/274-7232, fax/274-9524

Arizona
    SBDC, Maricopa County
    Community College
    2411 West 14th Street
    Tempe, AZ 85281-6941
    602/731-8720, fax/731-8729

Arkansas
    SBDC, University of Arkansas
    Little Rock Technology Center
        Building

100 South Main, #401
Little Rock, AR 72201
501/324-9043, fax/324-9049

California
    SBDC, California Trade &
    Commerce Agency
    801 K Street, #1700
    Sacramento, CA 95814
    916/324-5068, fax/322-5084

Colorado
    SBDC, Office of Business
    Development
    1625 Broadway, #1710
    Denver, CO 80202
    303/892-3809, fax/892-3848

Connecticut
    SBDC, University of Connecticut
    Box U-41, #422
    368 Fairfield Road
    Storrs, CT 06269-2041
    203/486-4135, fax/486-1576

Delaware
  SBDC, University of Delaware
  Pumell Hall #005
  Newark, DE 19711
  302/831-2747, fax/831-1423

District of Columbia
  SBDC, Howard University
  2600 6th Street NW, #128
  Washington, DC 20059
  202/806-1560, fax/806-1777

Florida
  SBDC, University of West Florida
  19 West Garden Street, 3rd Floor
  Pensacola, FL 32501
  904/444-2060, fax/444-2070

Georgia
  SBDC, University of Georgia
  Chicopee Complex
  1180 East Broad Street
  Athens, GA 30602
  706/542-6762, fax/542-6776

Hawaii
  SBDC, University of Hawaii
    at Hilo
  523 West Lanikaula Street
  Hilo, HI 96720
  808/933-3516, fax/933-3683

Idaho
  SBDC, Boise State University
  1910 University Drive
  Boise, ID 83725
  208/385-1640, fax/385-3877

Illinois
  SBDC, Department of Commerce
  & Community Affairs
  620 East Adams Street
  Springfield, IL 62701
  217/524-5856, fax/785-6328

Indiana
  SBDC, Economic Development
  Council
  One North Capitol, #420
  Indianapolis, IN 46204
  317/264-6871, fax/264-3102

Iowa
  SBDC, Iowa State University
  137 Lynn Ave.
  Ames, IA 50010
  515/292-6351, fax/292-0020

Kansas
  SBDC, Wichita State University
  1845 Fairmount
  Wichita, KS 67260-0148
  316/689-3193, fax/689-3647

Kentucky
  SBDC, University of Kentucky
  College of Business & Economics
  225 Bus. & Econ. Bldg
  Lexington, KY 40506-0034
  606/457-7668, fax/258-1907

Louisiana
  SBDC, Northeast Louisiana
  University
  College of Business Admin.
  700 University Ave.
  Monroe, LA 71209
  318/342-5506, fax/342-5510

Maine
  SBDC, University of Southern
  Maine
  96 Falmouth St.
  Portland, ME 04103
  207/780-4420, fax/780-4810

Maryland
  SBDC, Department of Economic &
  Employment Development
  217 E Redwood St., 9th flr
  Baltimore, MD 21202
  410/433-6995, fax/333-4460

Massachusetts
  SBDC, University of Mass.
  School of Mgmt, #205
  Amherst, MA 01003-4935
  413/545-6301, fax/545-1273

Michigan
  SBDC, Wayne State University
  2727 Second Ave.
  Detroit, MI 48201
  313/964-1798, fax/964-3648

Minnesota
SBDC, Dept. of Trade & Economic
Development
500 Metro Square
121 Seventh Place E
St. Paul, MN 55101-2146
612/297-5770, fax/296-1290

Mississippi
SBDC, University of Mississippi
Old Chemistry Building, 216
University, MS 38677
601/232-5001, fax/232-5650

Missouri
SBDC, University of Missouri
Suite 300, University Place
Columbia, MO 65211
314/882-0344, fax/884-4297

Montana
SBDC, Department of Commerce
1424 9th Ave.
Helena, MT 59620
406/444-4780, fax/444-2808

Nebraska
SBDC, University of Nebraska
at Omaha
60th & Dodge Streets
CBA room 407
Omaha, NE 68182
402/554-2521, fax/554-3747

Nevada
SBDC, University of Nevada
in Reno
College of Business
Administration, #411
Reno, NV 89557-0100
702/784-1770, fax/784-4347

New Hampshire
SBDC, University of New
Hampshire
108 McConnell Hall
Durham, NH 03824
603/862-2200, fax/862-4468

New Jersey
SBDC, Rutgers University
Ackerson Hall, 3rd Floor

180 University Street
Newark, NJ 07102
201/648-5960, fax/648-1110

New Mexico
SBDC, Santa Fe Community
College
P.O. Box 4187
Santa Fe, NM 87502-4187
505/438-1362, fax/438-1237

New York
SBDC, State University of
New York
SUNY Plaza S-523
Albany, NY 12246
518/443-5398, fax/465-4992

North Carolina
SBDC, University of
North Carolina
4509 Creedmoor Road, #201
Raleigh, NC 27612
919/571-4154, fax/571-4161

North Dakota
SBDC, University of
North Dakota
Gamble Hall, University Station
Grand Forks, ND 58202-7308
701/777-3700, fax/777-3225

Ohio
SBDC, Department of
Development
77 South High Street
Columbus, OH 43226-1001
614/466-2711, fax/466-0829

Oklahoma
SBDC, SE Oklahoma State
University
517 West University
Station A, Box 2584
Durant, OK 74701
405/924-0277, fax 924-7471

Oregon
SBDC, Lane Community College
99 West 10th Avenue, #216
Eugene, OR 97401
503/726-2250, fax/345-6006

Pennsylvania
SBDC, University of Pennsylvania
The Wharton School
444 Vance Hall
Philadelphia, PA 19104
215/898-1219, fax/573-2135

Puerto Rico
SBDC, University of Puerto Rico
Box 5253-College Station, Bldg. B
Mayaguez, PR 00681
809/834-3590, fax/834-3790

Rhode Island
SBDC, Bryant College
1150 Douglas Pike
Smithfield, RI 02917
401/232-6111, fax/232-6416

South Carolina
SBDC, University of South
Carolina
College of Business Admin.
1710 College Street
Columbia, SC 29208
803/777-4907, fax/777-4403

South Dakota
SBDC, University of
South Dakota
School of Business
414 East Clark
Vermillion, SD 57069
605/677-5498, fax/677-5427

Tennessee
SBDC, Memphis State University
South Campus, Getwell Road,
Bldg. 1
Memphis, TN 38152
901/678-2500, fax/678-4072

Texas
SBDC, University of Houston
1100 Louisiana, #500
Houston, TX 77002
713/752-8444, fax/756-1500

Texas
SBDC, University of Texas at
San Antonio
Cypress Tower, #410
1222 North Main Street
San Antonio, TX 78212
210/558-245 residual, fax/558-2464

Texas
SBDC, Texas Tech University
2579 South Loop 289, #114
Lubbock, TX 79423-1637
806/745-3973, fax/745-6207

Texas
SBDC, Dallas County Community
College
1402 Corinth Street
Dallas, TX 75215
214/565-5833, fax/565-5815

Utah
SBDC, University of Utah
102 West 500 South
Salt Lake City, UT 84101
801/581-7905, fax/581-7814

Vermont
SBDC, Vermont Technical College
P.O. Box 422
Randolph Center, VT 05060
802/728-9101, fax/728-3026

Virginia
SBDC, Department of Economic
Development
1021 East Cary Street
Richmond, VA 23206
804/371-8258, fax/371-8185

Virgin Islands
SBDC, Univ. of Virgin Islands
8000 Nisky Ctr, #202
Charlotte Amalie
St. Thomas, Virgin Islands
00802-5804
809/776-3206, fax/775-3756

Washington
SBDC, Washington State
University
College of Business & Economics
245 Todd Hall
Pullman, WA 99164-4727
509/335-1576, fax/335-0949

West Virginia
SBDC, Governor's Office of
Community & Industrial
Development
1115 Virginia Street East
Charleston, WV 25301
304/558-2960, fax/558-0127

Wisconsin
SBDC, University of Wisconsin
432 North Lake Street, #423
Madison, WI 53706
608/263-7794, fax/262-3878

Wyoming
SBDC, University of Wyoming
Wyoming Hall Room 414
P.O. Box 3922
Laramie, WY 82071-3922
307/766-3505, fax/766-3406

B

Minority Business Development Centers

Each of the Minority Business Development Agency Regional Offices listed here administers between thirteen and twenty-seven satellite offices operating as Minority Business Development Centers, Native American Business Development Centers, Minority Enterprise Growth Assistance Centers, Business Resource Centers, and Minority Business Opportunity Centers. The MBDA-funded centers are operated by private firms, nonprofit organizations, state and local government agencies, and educational institutions. Among other services, they identify private- and public-sector sources of financing for minority-owned firms and assist them with the preparation of financial documents and plans for submission to lenders.

Alaska, American Samoa, Arizona, California, Hawaii, Idaho, Nevada, Oregon, and Washington are serviced from:

MBDA Regional Office
221 Main Street, Room 1280
San Francisco, CA 94105
415/744-3001

Alabama, Florida, Georgia, Kentucky, Mississippi, North

Carolina, Puerto Rico, South Carolina, Tennessee, and the Virgin Islands are serviced from:

MBDA Regional Office
401 West Peachtree Street, NW, Suite 1715
Atlanta, GA 30308-3516
404/730-3300

Arkansas, Colorado, Louisiana, Montana, New Mexico, North

Dakota, Oklahoma, South Dakota, Texas, Utah, and Wyoming are serviced from:

MBDA Regional Office
1100 Commerce Street
Room 7B-23
Dallas, TX 75242
214/767-8001

Connecticut, Delaware, Maine, Maryland, Massachusetts, New Hampshire, New Jersey, New York, Pennsylvania, Rhode Island, Vermont, Virginia, Washington, DC,

and West Virginia are serviced from:

MBDA Regional Office
26 Federal Plaza, Room 3720
New York, NY 10278
212/264-3262

Illinois, Indiana, Iowa, Kansas, Michigan, Minnesota, Missouri, Nebraska, Ohio, and Wisconsin are serviced from:

MBDA Regional Office
55 East Monroe Street, Suite 1406
Chicago, IL 60603
312/353-0182

C

Resources

BUSINESS COUNSELING
AND REFERRALS

SBA Offices

To find special SBA offices (such as One-Stop Capital Shops and Microloan offices), SBDC, SCORE, or WBCD offices, or to inquire about SBA financing programs, you should call the SBA's 800 number:

800/8AskSBA   also 800/827-5722   or 202/653-7562

On the toll-free number, a recorded message prompts you to key in information to identify your questions, then it provides the information you need. For information on the SBA Disaster Program call 800/488-5323

SCORE Offices

For referral to a local office where you can find one-to-one counseling, business mentoring, or the networking round tables for women under the Women's Business Ownership program, call SCORE at:

800/634-0245

Other Assistance Centers

Information on other small-business assistance centers should be available from your county library. If this is not available at the general reference desk, then check with the business reference desk. You should also check your local telephone directory under state and federal government services for regional or community development centers. In many cities across the country, local chambers of commerce conduct small-business workshops, and some also have counseling and/or referral services. Entrepreneurial training programs may be found through local colleges and universities; some emphasize classroom work, others emphasize individual coaching.

ON-LINE SERVICES

SBA On-Line

Access SBA on-line for information on SBA publications and services, points of contact, calendars of local events, on-line training, access to other federal on-line services, electronic mail forums, Internet E-mail, special interest groups, and downloadable shareware files. SCORE can also be accessed on-line, through the SBA Home Page.

Data parameters:	300 - 19.2, N, 8, 1
1-800-697-4636:	SBA and other government agency information. Downloadable SBA information files and .QWK mail
1-900-463-4636:	SBA and other government agency information. 14 cents a minute.
	Downloadable shareware files
202/401-9600	Internet E-mail, DC Metro only
	On-line searchable databank
	Gateway
	Mail

Internet Telnet: www.sbaonline.sba.gov

202/205-6400:   Technical support

202/205-7333:   TDD

Site Seeing on the Internet

Uniform resource locators (URLs) are the addresses used to identify and access Home Pages on the Internet World Wide Web. Here are some URLs you may want to check out:

National Technical Information Service's FedWorld:
   http://www.fedworld.gov

Harvard's John F. Kennedy School of Government:
   http://ksgwww.harvard.edu/~ksgpress/ksgnews.htm

Patent and Trademark Office: http://www.uspto.gov

Department of Defense Procurement: http://www.acq.osd.mil/ec/

Securities and Exchange corporate filings (EDGAR):
   http://www.sec.gov/edgarhp.htm

The White House: http://www.whitehouse.government

MCI's Small Business Center—for tips and resources on financing, including venture capital, SBA lending, international trade financing, and more:
   http://www.mci.com

ANGEL NETWORKS

A number of universities, colleges, and economic development organizations maintain databases of private investors who are interested in small-business opportunities. These are privately run and are not affiliated with the SBA. If you contact any of them you should ask about charges, aging of the contacts, and the criteria for including listings on the databank. Do not assume that the organization maintaining the databank has verified the information or integrity of the listings. They are included for your information, without recommendation.

Los Angeles Venture Network (LAVN)
   213/743-1726
   University of Southern California
   Business Expansion Network

The Technology Capital Network
617/253-7163
Massachusetts Institute of Technology
(high-tech, agriculture, biotech, energy, and manufacturing)

The Capital Network
512/305-0826
University of Texas at Austin

Pacific Venture Capital Network
714/509-2990
University of California at Irvine
(high-tech and high-growth)

VENTURE CAPITAL

NASBIC
National Association of Small Business Investment Companies
1199 North Fairfax Street, Suite 200
Alexandria, VA 22314
703/683-1601

IVCI
International Venture Capital Institute
P.O. Box 1333
Stamford, CT 06904
203/323-3143

BIBLIOGRAPHY

Almanac of Business & Industrial Financial Ratios by Leo Troy (ed.). Prentice Hall, 800/223-2348.

Annual Statement Studies. Including comparative historical data and other sources of composite financial data. Disk or paperback. Robert Morris Associates, 800/677-7621.

Finding Private Venture Capital for Your Firm by Robert J. Gaston. John Wiley & Sons, 800/225-5945.

How to Borrow Money From a Banker: A Business Owner's Guide by Roger Bel Air. AMACOM, 800/262-9699.

Industry Norms & Key Business Ratios. Dun & Bradstreet, 800/526-0651.

Tax Savvy for Small Business by Frederick W. Daily. Nolo Press, 800/992-6656.

D

Protecting Your Business
from Disaster

Murphy's Law is alive and well and looking for new victims! Which is fair warning that if you don't take steps to help your business recover quickly from a disaster, yours will be the business most likely to suffer a disaster.

Disasters come in many forms—floods, hurricanes, earthquakes, and riots. And if you don't live in an area where any of those can occur, there are disgruntled employees, computer viruses, electrical spikes and outages, burst water mains, and fires in neighboring buildings along with the smoke and water that get everywhere when fires are being dowsed.

Fortunately, the biggest disaster of all is avoidable. *Because the biggest disaster of all is not to have taken steps to effect a speedy recovery in the event of any other kind of disaster.*

Disasters occur in varying degrees of severity, from the accident that erases an important computer file to the fire that destroys the entire physical location. The answer to fast recovery is to keep a complete historical record of your business off-site.

MAINTAINING BUSINESS
RECORDS OFF-SITE

What to include in your historical records depends on your type of business and your answer to the question: "If my business were destroyed by a disaster, what evidence would I need to get restitution from my insurance company and to arrange financing with my bank?"

Add your answers to the following list of suggestions:

- Insurance policies
- Lease or grant deeds on property
- Lease or purchase papers on machinery and equipment
- Copy of most recent inventory
- Loan papers
- Major contracts
- Customer database
- Bank accounts
- Tax returns
- Financial documents (balance sheets, income statements, cash flow sheets, budgets, etc.)
- Record of receivables
- Employee records, payroll and withholding tax records

When considering what to include, you can draw a distinction between the documents/information that are crucial and the documents/information that can be recovered from elsewhere. For instance, if you have copies of the title sheets of your insurance policies, tax returns, and loan papers, duplicates of the actual policies, tax returns, and loans can be obtained from the insurance companies, the IRS, and lenders. Similarly, provided you can identify each of your bank accounts quickly, duplicates of past statements may be obtained to verify which of your payables are still outstanding.

If your business is computerized, your task is easier, because you will only need to copy those papers that are not computerized. Of course, that's assuming you have a good computer backup system in place and operating. If you don't, start one *now*.

UPDATES

Assuming most of your business information, particularly your accounting, inventory, and marketing operations, are computerized, computer backups should take care of more than half the items on your list. The minimum backup and storage procedures of a good backup system will include the following:

1. **Daily Backups of Updated Files:** One copy on-site, or off-site but quickly accessible.

2. **Weekly Backups of All Current Data Files:** One copy on-site and a duplicate copy off-site. The previous week's backup should also be stored off-site.

3. **Monthly Backups of All Data Files:** Should be kept in an absolutely secure facility, such as a bank safe deposit box.

4. **Annual Backups of the Entire System:** At least two copies should be kept off-site; one should be kept in a bank safe deposit box and one should be kept out of the area along with the previous two or three full backups.

5. **Special Backups:** The annual off-site and out-of-area copies should be supplemented with the following:

   - Full backups of all *data* files when the annual accounting is completed and tax returns are filed
   - Full backups of all *system files both before and after* a system update
   - Full backups of all *data files both before and after* any major overhaul or purging of records
   - Full backup of all *data* files after any major changes in your data (such as after the addition of a major marketing plan or after your company does a mailing that results in significant additions to your customer database)

6. **Other Documents:** Documents that are not normally in your computer system may be scanned in so that they are preserved in the off-site backups. Otherwise, you need to implement a system whereby such documents are copied for off-site storage as needed.

STORAGE FACILITIES

Commercial storage facilities with varying degrees of security and levels of cost are available for the preservation of both paper and computer disks or tapes off-site. If you have a large volume of such material, commercial storage should be considered.

There are alternatives that easily meet the needs of small businesses.

- One copy of daily and weekly backup tapes or disks should be kept at your business because approximately 90 percent of access to such backups is to restore a single corrupted file. Most business owners store the duplicate daily and weekly backups at their homes, taking the chance that the need for the backups will be for a disaster at the business location, rather than one involving the entire area. Keeping daily and weekly backup duplicates in a bank safe deposit box is, for most of us, more onerous than is justified by the protection it would provide.

- It may seem simpler to entrust the off-site storage of computer backups to the person responsible for controlling the backups or to a company officer. However, if you do so it should only be after very careful consideration. This is your company, the backups contain your proprietary information, and the disks or tapes represent your blood, sweat, and tears. Don't enable anyone to lose, destroy, or steal their contents.

- Home-based businesses can provide themselves with off-site protection by sending the daily off-site copy to work with a spouse or by storing it in a detached garage or a car. One such owner takes his recent backups to his daughter's home whenever he visits; another home-business owner swaps tapes with a colleague at their weekly chamber meeting. Solutions that are simple and easy to carry out will probably be the most sustainable as a long-term habit.

- In the event of a major disaster, your annual and most recent month's backups will be used to restore your files and get you back into operation within hours. The ability to do this is surely worth the tedious monthly trek to a safe deposit box.

- Before-and-after backups are mandated whenever work on the system files or data files may cause the loss or corruption of a file. Before-and-after backups should be kept until they are obsolete, because data loss or corruption may not be immediately apparent.

- The out-of-area copies are additional insurance against Murphy's Law at its worst. Some business owners arrange to mail backups to commercial facilities on a monthly basis; others simply mail their packages to a family member in another state. You have to determine the degree of security, convenience, and cost that makes you most comfortable.

- Wherever you store your backups, they should be readily accessible when you need them.

STILL NOT CONVINCED?

If you are still not convinced regular computer backups are necessary here's what your peers are doing. In their April 1996 issue, Home Office Computing magazine announced that respondents to their survey report that 40 percent back up daily, 15 percent back up weekly, 10 percent back up bimonthly, and 35 percent back up monthly. And at least half of their survey respondents scan for viruses and defrag daily while most of the remainder do so monthly. Such regular attention to admittedly tedious tasks tells you that frequency should depend on your answer to the question: How much of my data would I lose if my computers were stolen or destroyed in the next 24 hours?

Glossary

Acid-test ratio Division of cash and accounts receivables by current liabilities.

Angels Individuals who invest in businesses through equity and/or loans.

Appreciation Increase in value of an asset.

Assets Value of cash, financial instruments, and goods owned.

Balloon loan Installment loan ending in a balloon payment.

Balloon payment Amount of principal due with final loan payment when a loan is not fully amortized (both principal and interest paid) in monthly payments.

Book depreciation Accounting practice (for tax purposes) of decreasing the ascribed value of assets according to a formula.

Break-even point Point where contribution margin is no longer needed for fixed costs and contributes to profit. Number of units needed to be sold to cover fixed costs.

Business cycle loan Loan made for the length of a business cycle and for the purpose of meeting the inventory or working capital costs incurred early in the cycle.

Capital Large sum of money used to finance a business. Amount of loan without interest.

Capital expenditure / investment / purchase Business possessions that are not sold or consumed in the course of business.

Collateral Possessions used to secure a loan, such as inventory, receivables, machinery, equipment, automobiles, financial instruments (stocks and bonds) and real estate.

Contribution margin Amount of sales price that remains after cost of goods is deducted, and contributes first to fixed costs and then to profit. *See* break-even point.

Convertible debentures *See* debentures.

Convertible preferred stock *See* stock.

Cosigner Someone who guarantees that you will repay the loan and who becomes liable for the balance if you don't.

Cost of goods sold Accounting term for purchase of supplies and direct costs of producing a product, or for the purchase of products for resale.

Current assets Liquid assets such as cash, bank accounts, accounts receivables, inventory, and prepaid expenses.

Current liabilities Those accounts that must be paid during the next twelve months.

Current ratio *See* working capital ratio.

Debentures, convertible Unsecured bonds that can be exchanged for stock, usually at the bondholder's option.

Depreciation Decrease in value of an asset. *See* book depreciation.

Due diligence The process of confirming each item in a business proposal and estimating the risks of an investment.

Equity Ownership.

Equity investments Capital invested by investors/stock owners.

Equity partners Investors who agree to split profits and responsibilities according to a formula that weighs capital, expertise, and the time and energy devoted to the enterprise.

Fixed assets Assets that are not converted to cash during normal operation.

Fixed-asset loan Loans made on physical assets such as equipment and machinery that become the loan's collateral.

Freehold Leased or owned facilities where business is located.

General expenses Goods that are consumed but don't contribute directly to the product or service, such as rent, stationery, and cleaning supplies.

Goodwill Value of a business beyond its physical and cash assets; the value of its customer base.

Gross profit Amount remaining from income after the cost of producing the product is deducted.

Guaranteed loan One that a cosigner (an angel or the SBA) guarantees will be paid.

Historical value Amount paid for an asset (usually one that appreciates).

Income Receipts from sales.

Industry averages Trends and ratios that are statistical averages for businesses in an industry.

Installment loan One of many names for the type of loan that is received in a lump sum and paid off in regular, usually monthly, installments.

Inventory funds Money for the purchase of supplies and direct costs of producing a product, or for the purchase of products for resale.

International letters of credit *See* letters of credit.

Letters of credit Letter from the bank that is a negotiable promise to pay on an international transaction.

Liabilities Amounts owed or committed in accounts payable, lease contracts, etc., and loans.

Line-of-credit Loan that can be drawn on to an agreed-upon limit in return for minimum monthly payments (charge cards).

Long-term liabilities Financial commitments beyond the next twelve months.

Market potential Portion or percent of a specific market at which the product or service is directed.

Net profit Amount remaining from income after the cost of producing the product and the cost of overhead are deducted.

Net worth Amount of equity; difference between assets and liabilities.

Operating capital *See* working capital.

Partnership, general Person involved in the daily management of the company and equally responsible for its debts.

Partnership, limited Person (investor) who has no say in the management of the company and cannot be held responsible for its debts.

Preferred stock *See* stock.

Profit Amount remaining from income after all expenses are paid.

Quick ratio *See* acid-test ratio.

Ratio of assets to debts The dollar value of assets compared to the dollar value of debts.

Risk capital *See* venture capital.

ROI Ratio for measuring return on investment.

Serial investment Investment by angel or venture capitalist that takes place in stages at timed intervals.

Second mortgage Real estate equity loan.

Secured loan Loan with collateral.

Seed money Early startup funds that cover a business or market plan or a product prototype.

Standard multiplier Accounting term for computing value with comparison to other businesses within an industry.

Stock, convertible preferred Ownership shares that enjoy special privileges, usually regarding dividend payments that can be exchanged for common stock at the holder's option.

Subordinated loans Loans that are paid back after any bank loan.

Supplies Items that go into your product or service.

Technical background Small business owner with a practical base of skills in turning out a specific product or service.

Term Length or life of a loan.

Term loan *See* installment loan.

Time of asset conversion Period of repayment of loan at end of business cycle when sales increase.

Venture capital Equity investment by individual or company who does not take a partnership position.

Voting control The right to vote and the weight of that vote (for example, an entrepreneur may keep 40 percent equity in a business but 51 percent voting control so that she or he can outvote the remaining stockholders).

Warrants, notes with Short-term debt instruments, usually due in less than five years, which carry provisions (warrants) allowing conversion into common stock under predetermined conditions.

Win-win Solutions to problems or negotiations in which both parties benefit.

Working capital Money to pay day-to-day expenses.

Working capital ratio Comparison of current assets and liabilities that indicates the solvency of a business.

Index